ALL IN

*Discovering the Love, Strength, and Blessings
God Gives to Those Who Are Faithful*

Dr. Marvin A. Jennings, Sr.

Renown Publishing
www.renownpublishing.com

All In / Marvin A. Jennings, Sr.
ISBN-13: 978-1-952602-61-0

Praise for *All In* by Marvin Jennings

When your conscience says you can't, Pastor Jennings' *All In* motivates readers to believe that, with God, everything is possible. *All In* offers excellent instruction that highlights the power of following God's plan for your life as the ultimate method for preordained greatness.

Beverly Walker-Griffea, Ph.D.
President, Mott Community College

Dr. Jennings book *All In* is a Spirit-filled motivational road map that will inspire you to take inventory of who you are and of your relationships with God and others as you journey through this life. It will cause you to grow as you go and bless others along the way. I would encourage anyone and everyone to read and seriously consider the reflections at the end of every chapter and to share this treasure with others, that they also will be truly blessed.

Cynthia Clarke
Grace Emmanuel Baptist Church

This book is dedicated to the glory, honor, and praise of God the Father and God the Holy Spirit. I thank God that by Him all things are possible and through Him this book has come to fruition. I thank God for each individual He has placed to foster, mentor, and encourage me and to enrich my life, my thinking, and most of all my spiritual development, growth, and direction.

I cannot mention every individual by name in this limited space, but please know I am eternally grateful. This book requires a special thanks to my devoted and charming love-goddess of fifty years, Janis, and to our adult children: Marvin, Jr., Micah, Celestine, Michella, and Calista (the cause of many joyous and Jesus moments). I am truly thankful and indebted to my late parents, Pastor Dr. James, Sr. and Mrs. Bertha Jennings of Detroit, Michigan, along with my late father- and mother-in-law, Deacon Abraham and Mrs. Gracie Knott.

To my siblings—my sisters, Delores and Evangelist Darlene, and my brothers, Bishop James, Jr., Pastor Dr. Everett, Sr., Minister Vincent, Pastor Harvey, Sr., and Pastor Patrick: as Apostle Paul stated, I rejoice with every remembrance of you for your contributions to my life's fabric and faith.
To Grace Emmanuel Baptist Church, as well as the late organizing Pastor Lindell L. Brady and Mrs. Peggy Brady: I'm overwhelmingly and eternally indebted to you, a very special church and a most loving and supportive congregation, whom I was blessed to have pastored for

over thirty-four years. Included in this tribute is a special thank-you to the administrative staff, who in no small measure helped to bring this to actualization: Mrs. Glenna Gates, Ms. Sheila Fowler, Deacon Wesley Thompson, Trustee Johnny Cowley, and Trustee Dr. James O. Shelley.

I am appreciative beyond words for the invaluable work, patience, and collaboration of Maria Floros (Chief of Staff) and the entire Speak It To Book / Sermon To Book organization for their deft, skillful proficiency and professionalism in compiling, publishing, and bringing to the public this printed-word proclamation of my sermons as a fabulous finished product.

CONTENTS

Deciding Whose Side You're On

Have you ever felt downtrodden, beaten up, lonely, and just plain miserable because you're living a life of faith in Jesus? Do you ask yourself if this is worth the time, the sacrifice, and everything you have given up while serving the Lord? Have you measured the cost of claiming the name of Jesus and being called a Christian? Have you asked yourself, "Is my faith really worth it?"

You're not alone.

But those who've said, "Lord, here I am" (see Isaiah 6:8), and have gone through the difficulties, scorn, and discrimination that come with the faith, have been lifted and transformed into something more beautiful and significant than they ever could have imagined. I can tell you honestly that with Jesus, I have never given up anything for which I didn't get more in exchange.

Sadly, there are too many folks sitting in church, under godly preaching, who haven't truly decided whose side they are on—whether they'll follow Jesus with their whole heart or go their own way. If you're one of the undecided, if you're still hanging out there on the fence, I want to help you see that following Him is worth it. I want to help you take inventory of your Christian self and understand the benefits that make this journey worthwhile.

KNOW WHO GOD IS

Faith is not about you. It's not about what you want, what you feel, or what you think. Faith starts with God and who He is. Too many people want to make a name for themselves (Genesis 11:4). But God already has the perfect name, and He is all that's needed. When you are in Christ, God gives you His name. God's name never fades. His character is perfect. His glory is our joy. If your name is found in His name, then you, too, will be lifted up.

A NEW KIND OF POWER

Are you looking to the cup of sin for comfort? Have you been taking out your hurt and anger on people who don't deserve it? Are you turning to the flesh to forget your troubles?

God wants to transform you by the power of His Holy Spirit, so stop trying to live in your old habits and your old self. Instead of looking to the pleasures and distractions of the world to satisfy you for the moment, bow your head and let the Holy Spirit fill you up for eternity. Every time you bow, you rise with a new revelation, a new power. It's a new you—renewed, invigorated, revised, and revitalized. In Him, you have access to unspeakable joy that the world cannot give you.

GOD BRINGS CLARITY

If you're sixty years old and still acting like you're twenty-five, and your life doesn't make sense to you, it's because you haven't made up your mind about which side you're on. You're trying to play it both ways, one foot in the Kingdom and one in the world, and now things are out of whack. Being a disciple of Jesus Christ gives your life meaning, focus, and direction. God teaches you to grow up as His follower so every day will make sense.

GOD REDEEMS YOUR PAST AND SECURES YOUR FUTURE

God forgives your wrongs and gives you a hope like no other. There are no more colorless dreams, tamed visions, reservations in giving, or small goals. This is the God of Abraham you serve. The God of Moses. The God of Elijah. He rose from the dead! You no longer need preeminence, position, popularity, praise, or any other earthly rewards. He is all you need.

GOD MAKES YOU UNASHAMED

There is a story about a young man in Rwanda who was murdered for his faith, and when his house was searched, a prayer he'd written was found in his office. It started with, "I'm part of a fellowship of the unashamed."[1] You have been born again as a child of the highest King. You are not ashamed. Sometimes you may go wrong and feel shame from it, but you won't stay wrong. Your Christian self will bring you back to God.

Just as this young man gave his life for Christ, you also will not hesitate in the face of sacrifice, flinch in the presence of the enemy, or meander in the maze of mediocrity. You will not waver when things don't go your way. You will not despair during stormy times. The young man's prayer also stated, "I won't give up, shut up, let up, until I have stayed up, stored up, prayed up, paid up, preached up for the cause of Christ."[2] Make this the declaration of your own life.

JESUS WILL UPHOLD YOU

When David was just a youth, he stood with the people of Israel and watched Goliath challenge them to a fight, one on one. When no one answered, the giant blasphemed Jehovah God, and David asked the seasoned fighters why no one rose to the challenge. King Saul was afraid to fight Goliath. Saul's son Jonathan was afraid to fight him. Everyone was afraid—everyone except David (1 Samuel 17).

When David marched onto that field to face the enemy with only a sling and five stones, he called out that the day would belong to God. Jehovah God would fight for him. David wasn't going to take God's glory, nor rely on his own power. And when David knocked down Goliath with the first stone, God raised David.

Our champion is coming, and His name is Jesus. All power in heaven and on earth is in His hands (Matthew 28:18). The battle belongs to Him (1 Samuel 17:47). Our mighty God made you with His fingers, together with the whole universe (Psalm 139:13). Imagine how much power there is when you're leaning on the everlasting arms of the Savior (Psalm 68:19)! His glory reaches above the earth, all the way into heaven (Psalm 57:5). He is all you need (John 6:35).

WHERE DOES YOUR ALLEGIANCE LIE?

You need to decide whose side you're on.

If you're on the Lord's side, you've got a *yes* inside you right now. If not, you have to make up your mind. If you're on God's side, you need to serve Him. He will keep you. He will walk with you. He will guide you. He will provide all you need.

If you want to be a disciple of Jesus, if you want to have a Christian self, if you want to do something with your life that you can't accomplish by your own power, then now is the time to cry out, "Lord, here I am." God will give you purpose, direction, and might. Nothing will be able to stop you.

This book will show you what a life lived in faith really looks like and how you can experience it. You will learn about the love, strength, and blessings God gives to those who are faithful. It will help reveal to you the character of Jehovah God. And at the end of each chapter, application-focused workbook sections and action steps will guide you toward a deeper understanding of living for Christ in *your* daily walk with Him.

Now continue reading and explore how God can transform your life!

CHAPTER ONE

God-Given, God-Driven Love

In 1984, a hit song by Tina Turner posed in unforgettable terms (and perhaps unintentionally) one of the most profound questions of human existence: "What's love got to do with it?"[3]

And here is the truth we too often miss: love has everything to do with it. First Corinthians 13:13 tells us, in the King James Version, "And now abideth faith, hope, charity, these three; but the greatest of these is charity." The New King James Version translates "charity" as "love." If you're looking for meaning in your life—if you're looking for purpose—you need to look to love, because love is what will last.

Maybe right now, you're thinking about your life and the world around you and wondering how the Bible can claim that love lasts. Maybe there are divisions in your family: children who are rebelling against their parents, brothers who have parted in anger, spouses who won't even speak to each other. Maybe you've experienced divorce. Maybe you had a close friend who betrayed you.

This world likes to sing about love and sell love on television and in magazines, but the reality we see is love going wrong. Divorce rates are up. People fall out of love. People use each other. People turn on each other. Sometimes people give up on love altogether and believe they can rely only on themselves. People are lonely. People are angry. People are hurt.

We need to understand that the love Paul was writing about in 1 Corinthians 13 is not the same love as what the world offers. He wasn't talking about the kinds of love that come naturally to us as human beings. Paul didn't use the word *eros*. He wasn't talking about passionate or romantic love. He didn't use the word *philia* for brotherly love or friendship. And he didn't use the word *storge*, which is devotional love for your family or country.[4]

We know those types of love don't last. Love like that will come and go. Sometimes we feel it, and sometimes we don't. Sometimes we'll say, "I love you," and not even mean it. These kinds of love might bring people together, but they can't be relied on to keep people together. No, the kind of enduring love that Paul was writing about, the kind that can stand up against anything, is *agape*, God's perfect love for mankind.

Godly love will never go bad. It will never turn on you. It is matchless, immeasurable, and incomprehensible. There's a power in it that's not of this world. It doesn't come from us. It's something we have to be given by its originator, the Holy God of the universe. He is the one who shows us what true love is.

When you give your life to Christ and decide to follow Him, the love you need to concern yourself with is God's kind of love. A life lived on faith is a life lived with God-given, God-driven love. Wherever you go and whatever you do as part of your Christian walk, it all starts with God's love, and God's love is what will sustain it. God loves us even though we don't deserve His love and could never earn it. His love is His supreme gift to us, and through His Word, He teaches us how to share this love with other people.

GOD'S PERFECT LOVE

So then, what does this God-given, God-driven love look like? First Corinthians 13 gives us a detailed description:

> *Charity suffereth long, and is kind; charity envieth not; charity vaunteth not itself, is not puffed up, doth not behave itself unseemly, seeketh not her own, is not easily provoked, thinketh no evil; rejoiceth not in iniquity, but rejoiceth in the truth; beareth all things, believeth all things, hopeth all things, endureth all things. Charity never faileth...*
>
> **—1 Corinthians 13:4–8a**

Chances are, you're thinking, "You've got to be kidding. This is way beyond me. It's not even possible!" Remember, God's love doesn't come naturally to us. In many ways, it goes against fallen human nature. That's why God has to spell it out for us. He has to tell us and show us what true love is.

11

Godly love is patient, kind, and consistent. It's not here today and gone tomorrow. It's not one way in public and another way behind closed doors. When you love someone with godly love, you love them even when it's difficult. You love them even when you feel tired, stressed, and irritable. You love them when they get on your nerves. If they are mean to you, you are still kind to them. You never try to make an excuse for not loving someone; you simply love them, no matter what.

Agape means loving people you don't necessarily like. You love people even when they don't look or act like you think they should. You love people who don't have it all together. You love people who have messed up big time.

That's the love we need from God, right? Christ gave His life for the unworthy, and that includes you. God loves us at our Sunday best and our Wednesday worst, and every one of us would be in trouble if He didn't.

Godly love is also unselfish. It's not about taking other people to task for wounding your pride. It's not about getting your own or getting even. It's not about making yourself look good. It's not about what you want or what other people can do for you. It's about looking to other people's needs. It's about giving your best when you may not get anything in return. It's about sacrifice.

In Romans 5:8, we read, "But God commendeth his love toward us, in that, while we were yet sinners, Christ died for us." Jesus Christ gave everything of Himself to people who didn't deserve it and never would. That is our standard for love. If we have anything we can boast or glory in, it's the cross (Galatians 6:14).

Don't be overwhelmed or intimidated. Don't give up before you begin because you think loving like this is out of your reach. God doesn't just say, "Do this," and then leave you to fail at it. He is the one who is going to enable you to love like He does. You can't give godly love unless you first get it from God Himself. God deposits His love in you for the benefit of other people. You are not at the helm; God is. He will step into you and love other people through you.

This doesn't mean *agape* won't be hard for you. God will direct you to love the unlovely, the downtrodden, the hopeless, and the heartbroken, even when you don't feel like it. It will be inconvenient and uncomfortable. Sometimes you won't understand it. But keep going. Let go of your prejudices, your preconceptions, and your agenda, and let God do His loving work through you. This is God's will for your life. This is what He wants for His people. And when you are personally, intimately connected with God, it will become what you want, too.

THE MAN IN THE PIT

Consider the following illustration of how God's love compares to human attitudes:

A SUBJECTIVE person came along and said: "I feel for you down there."

An OBJECTIVE person came along and said: "It's logical that someone would fall down there."

A CHRISTIAN SCIENTIST came along: "You only think that you are in a pit."

A PHARISEE said: "Only bad people fall into a pit."

A MATHEMATICIAN calculated how he fell into the pit.

A NEWS REPORTER wanted the exclusive story on his pit.

A FUNDAMENTALIST said: "You deserve your pit."

CONFUCIUS said: "If you would have listened to me, you would not be in that pit."

BUDDHA said: "Your pit is only a state of mind."

A REALIST said: "That's a pit."

A SCIENTIST calculated the pressure necessary (lbs./sq.in.) to get him out of the pit.

A GEOLOGIST told him to appreciate the rock strata in the pit.

AN EVOLUTIONIST said: "You are a rejected mutant destined to be removed from the evolutionary cycle." In other words, he is going to die in the pit so that he cannot produce any "pit-falling" offspring.

The COUNTY INSPECTOR asked if he had a permit to dig a pit.

A PROFESSOR gave him a lecture on "the elementary principles of the pit."

An EVASIVE person came along and avoided the subject of his pit altogether.

A SELF-PITYING person said: "You haven't seen anything until you've seen my pit!"

A CHARISMATIC said: "Just confess that you're not in a pit!"

An OPTIMIST said: "Things could be worse!

A PESSIMIST said: "Things will get worse."

JESUS, seeing the man, took him by the hand and lifted him out of the pit.[5]

The world will ignore, dismiss, reject, judge, and condemn you, but when you turn to God, He will reach right down to where you are and pull you out. In Psalm 40:2, David said, "He brought me up also out of an horrible pit, out of the miry clay; and set my feet upon a rock, and established my goings."

God's love for you is unfailing and undying. He has done for you things that no one else would have or could have done. God lifted you out of the pit of sin and destruction and despair. He gave you His best love when you were at your worst, and now you stand on Christ, the solid Rock. You have a high, strong place to stand on, where you can't be shaken, and God is asking you to look around you for other people who need to be lifted up. Love like that is powerful. Love like that can and will change the world.

Chapter One Questions

Question: There are four Greek words—*eros, philia, storge,* and *agape*—that are translated as *love* in English. What is agape love, and how is it different from the others?

_____

_____

_____

_____

_____

_____

_____

_____

_____

_____

_____

Question: Which part of the definition of love in 1 Corinthians 13 do you find the most challenging? When have you given or received this type of love, and how did it affect you?

_____

_____

_____

_____

_____

_____

_____

_____

_____

_____

_____

Question: *You can't give godly love unless you first get it from God Himself.* How do you know that God loves you? What would you say to a person who says, "God could never love someone like me"? What would you say to a believer who knows that God loves them, but struggles to live in the reality and power of His unconditional love?

_____

_____

_____

_____

_____

_____

_____

_____

_____

_____

_____

Action: What is your pit story? When did God rescue you, deliver you, and show you His love? Do you know someone who is stuck in a pit right now and needs a reminder of God's love? Share your story with them this week.

Chapter One Notes

_____

_____

_____

_____

_____

_____

_____

_____

_____

_____

_____

_____

_____

_____

_____

God Knows Best

Moses lived a remarkable life. I am sure at the end of his life, he looked back at a considerable number of significant memories. He grew up in Pharaoh's courts (Exodus 2). He stood barefoot before the Great I Am, who spoke from the burning bush (Exodus 3). He asked the Egyptian ruler to let his people, the Israelites, go free. He was God's mouthpiece as the ten plagues were unleashed on Egypt (Exodus 4:16 NLT).

He must have recalled the parting of the Red Sea and meeting God on the mountain to accept the commandments—as well as his people's constant backsliding and rejection of God, and the forty years walking through the wilderness. He was sure to remember the times when he pleaded with God not to destroy Israel (Deuteronomy 9:18–29).

Yet Moses sinned, too, and so he was not allowed to enter the Promised Land (Numbers 20:10–13).

Do you think Moses looked back on his life and said,

"Well, that was a waste," because of the mere fact that he did not get to cross into the Promised Land? Or do you think he was able to see the incredible plan of God unfolding throughout his life?

Think back on a situation where it seemed like nothing was going well for you. Did you see that God had a plan for you, but when you tried to go through the door He opened, you found the going so difficult that you wanted to give up? Or perhaps you felt you were following God's direction, yet you found yourself logically and logistically going the wrong way.

It's not just you. I have experienced the same thing. And your other Christian brothers and sisters have been in that boat, too.

Sometimes it's hard to keep up with what God is doing, because we don't have the full picture. We can't always see how things will work out. But I've learned that trusting God to guide us, even when it's difficult, is our sure way to a glorious future. He always knows the best way to take us.

ALL IN GOOD TIME

Let's face it: trusting God can be tough when the worries and demands of this world take over. Paying the bills and feeding your family are consuming more and more resources. Many times, the paycheck or available funds don't seem like they will stretch to meet all the needs.

Philippians 4:19 says, "But my God shall supply all your need according to his riches in glory by Christ Jesus." God has riches, and He would like to share them with you. He cares for the poor and the oppressed. His path may not lead you to a mansion or a dozen expensive cars. Maybe it will, but regardless, God is able and willing to care for you.

In Psalm 84:11–12, we read, "For the LORD God is a sun and shield; the LORD will give grace and glory; no good thing will He withhold from those who walk uprightly. O LORD of hosts, blessed is the man that trusteth in thee." When we are on God's side, He provides for us and blesses us abundantly. He lights our path so we can see which way to go, and He shields us from the enemy (Psalms 18:30 and 119:105). He rewards those who keep the faith and diligently seek Him.

God has things prepared for you that you don't even know about, blessings that you can't even imagine. All He asks is that you walk with Him in righteousness and let Him guide you. Then He will provide you with resources, opportunities, and relationships that you never thought would come your way. He will take you down unexpected paths with surprising twists and turns and lead you to a future of true fulfillment.

Maybe you're looking at your life right now and thinking that God must have forgotten about you. Where is your blessing? Where is your shining moment to bask in God-given glory?

Consider this reason that God gave for His choice of path for the newly liberated Israelites: "And it came to pass, when Pharaoh had let the people go, that God led them not through the way of the land of the Philistines, although that was near; for God said, Lest peradventure the people repent when they see war, and they return to Egypt" (Exodus 13:17).

Although the distance to the Promised Land was only a two-week hike through the land of the Philistines, God knew the Israelites weren't ready to face this enemy. He turned them away from the quicker path to help them grow in obedience, love, and faith.

God is concerned with your journey as well as your destination. If you are walking in relationship with Him, it means He is with you every step of the way. God brought you to the place where you are now in your life. Even this moment, in which you and I are communicating through the lines on this page, was orchestrated by God from the beginning. He has a purpose for every season, so trust Him to lead you at all times and to accomplish His work in and through you.

DETOURS

Sometimes God reveals His purpose to you and puts in your heart something He intends to do with your life. Then you eagerly and joyfully charge forth to receive it, only to come up against a brick wall before you reach the goal. At these times, you may wonder if God really knows what He is doing. You were pursuing His purpose for you, so what was wrong with the way you were going?

Just as God led the children of Israel away from the land of the Philistines, sometimes He will take you on a detour. You may feel like you're heading in the wrong direction, away from your destination, but God is still at work. If God is taking you on an alternate route, He may be doing it to keep you away from your own "Philistines": people or situations that may harm you emotionally, spiritually, or physically. Even if this new path takes longer than you thought or looks completely different from what you expected, you need to trust Him. God knows what He is doing, where He is taking you, and why He is taking you that way.

One important part of God's character to keep in mind is that He knows you intimately. He knows your thoughts, your desires, and your weaknesses (1 John 3:20). He knows what you can handle. He knows the trials that will help prepare you for what you will face in the future. He knows the blessings you need. He knows when you're tired, hungry, lonely, or frustrated. He sees when people are cruel to you.

In 1 Corinthians 10:13, Paul wrote, "There hath no temptation taken you but such as is common to man: but God is faithful, who will not suffer you to be tempted above that ye are able; but will with the temptation also make a way to escape, that ye may be able to bear it." Sometimes you think you're ready for a job promotion or a bit of fame or some extra cash, but God knows you're not ready, because He knows you won't be able to handle the struggle that comes with added responsibility. You need to learn how to trust God's guidance and His timing.

God shepherds you through temptation, but what about trials? Is it safe to trust that He knows the best way for you to go through the hardest of times?

Absolutely, yes! He guided the Israelites with a cloud of dust by day and a pillar of fire by night, and He will guide you through the wilderness, where there are no roads or paths to follow. Whenever you don't know what to do and you need divine guidance, inspiration, illumination, or insight, the Lord will take over if you let Him. God leads you like a good shepherd, beside still waters, in pleasant valleys, and even through the valley of the shadow of death. He is there, continually leading you, and you never have to fear evil when you are with Him (Psalm 23:4). He will guide you away from anyone and anything that could steal from your destiny and rob you of what He has for you.

WRONG TURNS

It's true that God may lead you along unexpected paths, but sometimes the change of direction is your own doing. You may have had moments when you chose the desires of the flesh over God's will. You may have forsaken your faith and tried to work things out for yourself. And of course, there was the time before you belonged to Him, when sin ruled your life. The question is: will your wrong turns prevent God from leading you to your destiny?

Let's again consider the Israelites. They deeply disappointed God when they erected a golden calf to worship. He wanted to destroy them and start over with Moses (Deuteronomy 9:13–14), but Moses asked God to have mercy and not destroy them (Deuteronomy 9:18–29).

Jesus does the same for us when we mess up. If we repent and ask God for forgiveness, "he is faithful and just to forgive us our sins, and to cleanse us from all unrighteousness" (1 John 1:9). If we turn back to God, He has promised not to turn us away.

This is true even when our past sins are truly terrible. Take David, for example. He looked upon Bathsheba in lust, slept with her, impregnated her, and then arranged for her husband to be killed. Imagine how grieved God was over David's actions! But David, heartbroken over how he had wronged God, repented. He did what he could to make things right on earth, and he humbled himself before God and asked for forgiveness.

All of David's sins—and there were far more than his affair with Bathsheba—were not enough to keep God from loving him. While there were horrible consequences for David's actions, God still called him "a man after mine own heart" (Acts 13:22). Even after David messed up big-time, his friendship with God could be restored.

We all have wrong turns in our past, but God won't let those seal our future. When you give your life to God, He stands between you and your yesterday. He will lead you away from the sins that would hurt you, keep you captive, and prevent you from reaching your destiny.

IT TAKES TWO

God will lead you and protect you on all sides, but He won't do the walking for you. He won't teleport you through space and time to your blessed future. He will guide your feet, but you have to take the steps.

When the children of Israel left Egypt, they walked through the desert and wandered through the wilderness.

They stepped out in faith, believing that God would take care of them. They walked through trials, sometimes failing, other times seeing God's majesty and power first-hand. And, as a nation, they made it to the Promised Land.

What if the Israelites had just sat around, twiddling their thumbs? What if they had talked about going but never actually left? What if they had decided their houses were too comfortable and their jobs too nice (they weren't) to follow the leading of God?

Don't mistake God's promise to guide you for a guarantee that He will do all the work while you kick back and relax. God will enable you to do what you need to do, but you need to do it. Use the resources available to you to travel from where you are to where God wants you to be. The plans are in place, and the road has been laid out for you (Jeremiah 29:11). It's time to get moving.

God won't reward laziness and slothfulness. He isn't going to move you like a puppet. He has given you free will, and He expects you to use it. Your journey with God takes two; it's a relationship between you and Him. You need to invest in the partnership and work with Him.

But, at the same time, don't forget where the blessings come from: "Every good gift and every perfect gift is from above and cometh down from the Father of lights" (James 1:17a). When you are following God and He blesses you, the danger is that your pride may sneak in and tempt you to give yourself the credit. Never forget that God is the source of all the good things in your life. All of your achievements have occurred because it is God who guides, equips, and protects you. He leads you and walks with you in your daily living. You couldn't be where you are without Him.

If you are a Christian, your life is not about you. You will be blessed, but you need to use every blessing as an opportunity to glorify God. He is the one who gives you the opportunities, talents, skills, and resources to succeed. He will decide how and when to bless you.

God will accomplish what He plans for your life. He will lead you in a way that brings you to where He wants you in the manner He knows is best. He is working in your life for His glory. He will take your brokenness and make you whole again. He will take your wounds and cause you to shout for joy. He will exalt you to a higher level and carry you to a future of eternal blessing that is beyond anything you could ever achieve or even imagine for yourself.

Trust in God and don't be afraid. He has proven Himself over and over again. If God has made a promise, it's already done. He is able, and He is faithful. You couldn't be in better hands.

Chapter Two Questions

Question: Describe a time in your life that was confusing, difficult, or dangerous to go through, yet you are able to look back on now and appreciate the truth that God knows best. What is a current situation in your life in which it is hard to trust God?

_____

_____

_____

_____

_____

_____

_____

_____

_____

_____

_____

Question: What are some of the possible reasons for God's "detours" or extended periods of waiting?

_____

_____

_____

_____

_____

_____

_____

_____

_____

_____

_____

Question: When have you made a wrong turn and gotten off God's path for you? How should a believer respond when they realize they have diverted from God's will?

_____

_____

_____

_____

_____

_____

_____

_____

_____

Action: Divide a piece of paper into two columns. Label one column "God's Responsibility" and the other "My Responsibility." Think about your response from the first question. What has God promised to do, and for what are you waiting on Him? Write those things in the column, "God's Responsibility." What is God asking you to do, and what steps of obedience do you need to take? Write those in the column, "My Responsibility."

Chapter Two Notes

_____

_____

_____

_____

_____

_____

_____

_____

_____

_____

_____

_____

_____

_____

_____

_____

Your Best Life—If You Want It

Abraham Lincoln, as a man, was tall, skinny, and ugly. He came from a poor family and had to fight for every opportunity that came his way. So, how did a man who was born in a one-room log cabin become the leader of a nation?[6]

Lincoln's image is carved upon Mount Rushmore for an important reason: his contribution to humanity earned him recognition as one of America's greatest presidents. America was split in two, and Lincoln found himself on one side of a country fighting a civil war. He saw it as his destiny to take the offensive in reuniting the country.

In the South, meanwhile, as people cried for freedom, Lincoln understood that he couldn't truly free the enslaved people in America with the flourish of a pen. They had to claim the freedom for themselves—which the freed men and women did. Lincoln's genius was to pave a road for the slaves. Using a combination of politics and war, of eloquence and action, he showed America the first steps in righting a terrible sin.

God uses people in adverse circumstances to do great things. Just look at other highly successful people from various walks of life, such as Sir Walter Scott, John Bunyan, George Washington, Franklin D. Roosevelt, Ludwig Beethoven, Harry Truman, and George Washington Carver. Psychologists Victor and Mildred Goertzel studied four hundred successful people like these and found that "of the 400, a full 75%—some 300 individuals—had grown up in a family burdened by a severe problem: poverty, abuse, absent parents, alcoholism, serious illness or some other misfortune."[7]

What did these men and women have in common? Regardless of circumstances, they wanted to be the best they could be. God wants you to reach your potential, too, and climb to higher heights. But first you must have a powerful desire to do something worthwhile with your life. You must have "a want to."

Do you have a dream for your life, a desire in your heart? Have you thought to yourself, "I can't make it, I can't achieve my dream," because of your background, circumstances, or environment? Have you been afraid to start down the path of your dream because the journey seems too daunting? Have you been so discouraged that you've given up in the face of difficulty?

If so, that's not what God intends. When He gives you a dream, He will enable you to achieve it if you trust Him enough to pursue it. He can use you, no matter your background, your circumstances, or your weaknesses. Don't reject the work and the blessings that He has in store for you.

Remember, God knows best. If He has put a dream or a purpose in your heart, it's not by accident. He has chosen you.

There's more good news: God has blessed you with all you need to start your journey. True, there will be hard work ahead, and both joy and discouragement, but there is a wonderful bounty in your life. You can be all God says you are, and you can accomplish all that God has designed for you.

But you have to *want to*.

REFUSING TO SETTLE

Abraham Lincoln was a lawyer, but he didn't go to school to learn how to argue in courts. Instead, he read books on his own time and took the exam to be a lawyer. That was quite a feat, and being a successful lawyer is a worthy goal—but it would have been only the second-best life for Lincoln.

Lincoln didn't just sit back and enjoy his status as a successful lawyer and local politician. He kept working in politics to try to make changes that would help others, including those who were less fortunate. His skills in debate were sharpened, and people would drive from far and wide to hear him speak. Eventually, those people voted him into the White House, where he helped reshape a nation.

God has made you wonderfully special and different. Don't scale down your value to fit in with the crowd and be average. Don't exchange your God-given gifts for second-class friendships. Don't allow the daily grind of life to fool you into thinking there's nothing more for you than just getting by. Like Abraham Lincoln, keep striving to be your best self.

To make sure you're not settling for average, you must ask some uncomfortable questions of yourself: Are your gifts going to waste in the Lord's house? Are you sitting in the pew for worship and God's preaching, then heading home without contributing? Your gifts are to be used in God's house as well, not merely to help you skate by in life.

Colossians 3:23 says, "And whatsoever ye do, do it heartily, as to the Lord, and not unto men." Keep honing your skills and developing your gifts. Use your talents in church, not just at your day job. Put your heart into everything that you do, and don't sell yourself short. God has given you something unique to contribute to the body of Christ and to the world. If something is getting in the way of you pushing past average, find out, knock it out, and move forward. Whatever those challenges are, they're not bigger than God.

One key to moving past mediocrity is never losing sight of your own possibilities. God doesn't hide your talents from you, and He especially doesn't hide them from loving family members. If everyone you know says you have a beautiful singing voice, and you love singing, why are you hiding your gift away? Don't just make a joyful noise at home and in the shower. Sing God's praises on the highest mountain! Use your voice in church and in the world to bring Him glory.

Daniel, in the Old Testament, was snatched away from his home in Israel and sold into slavery. He was forced to serve a king who didn't believe in God (Daniel 1:3–6). But he never lost faith, and he never lost a grip on the possibility that God had more planned for him than a life of slavery (Daniel 6:21–

22).

Daniel 1:4 gives us insight into what King Nebuchadnezzar was looking for in his slaves: "young men in whom there was no blemish, but good-looking, gifted in all wisdom, possessing knowledge and quick to understand, who had ability to serve in the king's palace, and whom they might teach the language and literature of the Chaldeans" (nkjv).

It wasn't enough for Daniel to be a scholar, to impress his captors, or even to have the king's approval. He remained faithful to God: "Daniel purposed in his heart that he would not defile himself with the portion of the king's meat, nor with the wine which he drank" (Daniel 1:8). He chose to honor God instead of adopting the practices of the culture around him.

Was it easy? I'm guessing it was as hard as watching everyone around you eating cinnamon rolls if you're trying to lose weight or can't eat gluten. Daniel must have stuck out like a sore thumb when the easier and safer thing to do would have been to blend in. But God had big plans for Daniel: he was to be councilor to a king. It was a good thing Daniel didn't settle for second best but kept himself ready for the amazing things that God would do through him.

If you think that your life is limited to your current circumstances, think again! The best that God has for you is more than you could imagine, so don't settle for less.

NO EXCUSES WITH GOD AT YOUR SIDE

One reason why rising above mediocrity is so challenging is that when you step out on faith and use your gifts, Satan isn't going to sit by and watch. Family members and friends may recognize your gifts, but the people close to you also have a way of speaking to your doubts. "Oh, you do have a lovely voice, but let's not take this too far," your parent might say when you're thinking of entering a singing contest. "Did you have to sing *that* song in the service? I don't really care for it," a church member might comment. While these might not be direct attacks from Satan, they sure feel like it.

God didn't say it would be easy, but He did say, "I am with you." Even in the worst of circumstances, He is by your side. Don't be intimidated by the obstacles in your path or your own weaknesses. God works best when you are feeling your worst, which simply means you are in need of less "self" and more God (see 2 Corinthians 12:9). After all, if everything is in your favor, you're not a candidate for a miracle.

Another challenge with stepping out on faith to use your gifts is how much energy it takes to keep going. We grow tired. Even Jesus was tired as He looked to rest after a few days of preaching (Mark 6:30–33). However, when He saw the crowds, He had compassion on them and continued to preach, and no doubt many more believed in Him (Mark 6:34).

When energy is low, try to rest. When you're tired and cannot rest, Satan brings discouragement. But remember also that Jesus says, "I am with you," and He will give you strength

(Matthew 28:20).

"I can't" is a powerful excuse that stops many people short of the life God intends for them. With Jesus, there is no "can't." As Paul wrote, "I can do all things through Christ which strengtheneth me" (Philippians 4:13). "Can't" won't do anything for you—or for God—but He will do anything for you if it aligns with His plans.

DON'T WORRY AND DON'T QUIT

Never waste a moment of your life worrying about whether God will be there for you. That's not in question, because He will stop short of nothing to take care of you. Jesus went so far as to sacrifice Himself on the cross to save us— not because He had to, but because He wanted to. Remember Philippians 4:19, "But my God shall supply all your need according to his riches in glory by Christ Jesus."

There is no question that God will take care of you. What's in question is your commitment. The key to realizing your potential is a simple desire and drive. The opportunity is there. The path is prepared. But you need to be willing to take it.

Reverend Allan C. Oggs, Sr. was a man who said, "You gotta have the want to."8 He was born with cerebral palsy, and doctors gave him no hope of becoming a functioning human being. He would be blind, they said, and unable to walk or talk—if he even survived. Doctors suggested that his parents pray for him to die young, a merciful death, so he wouldn't have to suffer through life.

Instead, his parents prayed for a miracle. They worked with specialists to help the boy cope with his physical disabilities. While other children learned to walk, Allan learned to stumble and fall. "Don't pick him up if he's not injured," doctors said. "Make him learn to get up on his own." So the boy staggered to his feet on his own.

Allan's words came out slurred, but with work, he made himself understood to others. When he went to school, Allan noticed that the kids never laughed at him.

After his parents bought him an Erector set and he started work on a construction project, Allan experienced spasms that sent nuts and bolts flying. He crawled on his hands and knees to pick them up. He held up the nut, looked squarely at it, and said, "You think you're going to get away from me? I'm going to screw you down so tight your ears hurt." Looking back on this episode later in life, he would reflect that it was a case of one nut talking to another nut.

When Allan's mother reluctantly agreed to let him have a bicycle, he crashed repeatedly. Day after day, he bled and bruised with little to no progress—until one day, it worked. He balanced himself and was able to go some distance before he fell. He continued to ride his bicycle often. Sometimes he would fall, but he wouldn't let the occasional, painful setback stop him.

Allan never let his disability get in the way of his sense of humor or his "want-to." He didn't let the things that slowed him down stop him completely. He chose to keep fighting.

That same attitude led Allan, the boy who was supposed to die, to college. When spasms kept him from buttoning his shirt, tying his tie, or shaving, his roommates helped him. He couldn't take notes, but he passed his courses and graduated after three years.

Despite all of the odds, Allan C. Oggs became a pastor and preached for over thirty years. He became a vice president of Jackson College of Ministries in Jackson, Mississippi, a board member, and a homiletics instructor. This life of purpose, achievement, and fulfillment was possible because he had the "want to" and he had God at his side—a combination more powerful than anything that stepped in his way.

Too often, people give up for reasons far smaller than the obstacles Allan Oggs faced. Don't give up on the amazing life God has planned for you! Though you may fall and take your lumps at times, continue to walk your journey with Jesus. Messing up, encountering difficulties, and feeling that the whole world is against you are not excuses. The world and the enemy may be against you, but God is with you, so take courage and keep trying.

NO MORE SITTING AROUND

I wanted to go to college and be a preacher. My high school counselor insisted that I learn a trade instead, and electrical school sounded good. Yet the Lord opened up a path to go to college, and though the counselor wasn't keen on the idea, I went anyway. Now I don't have one degree—I have three!

I'm not bragging, because I'm not bright. God saw someone unworthy of a blessing, someone unqualified, and said to me, "I can do something with you. Do you want to?" I did want to, because sitting around wasn't good enough for me. Now I'm a pastor, living the full life of joy that God intended for me. I didn't accept a safe job as an electrician because that would have been second best.

Just thinking big dreams doesn't give you a "want to." Trusting God and His plan for you means you also need a plan. Like Abraham Lincoln, Allan Oggs, and me, you need to devise a plan that will work in your circumstances. If you need a job, sitting at home and saying, "God will work it out," isn't the answer. You need a plan, and you need to follow it. Put it into practice. If God is calling you to college, make a plan to get there, even if you take one night-class a semester while you work a job. Eventually, you will finish.

When you make up your mind to do things God's way, He will stand with you. He will walk with you. He will help you. This will happen regardless of your circumstances, your environment, your color or ethnicity, or your prior education. If you have the "want to," God can help you do anything that's worthy of Him and His design for you. If you have a plan and put it into action, God will direct your steps (Proverbs 16:9 nasb).

The Lord enables you to live encouraged, equipped, and empowered. He helps you to grow into your potential and live your best possible life. You just have to want to do it.

Chapter Three Questions

Question: Who is a person (from either past or present) whom you admire for their persistence in overcoming difficulty and making a difference in the world?

_____

_____

_____

_____

_____

_____

_____

_____

_____

_____

_____

Question: What are your gifts, talents, and abilities? What dream has God put in your heart about how He wants to use them?

_____

_____

_____

_____

_____

_____

_____

_____

_____

_____

Question: What are some of the obstacles you may face as you step forward in faith to fulfill God's plan for your life? What are some truths that can keep you from giving up or settling for mediocrity?

_____

_____

_____

_____

_____

_____

_____

_____

_____

_____

_____

Action: "If you have a plan and put it into action, God will direct your steps." Think back on the dream that you have of using your gifts and abilities to glorify God. What is your plan for making this dream a reality—and have you taken action, or does it remain only a dream? Write out three specific goals, and then take those first steps to seeing God fulfill your dream!

Chapter Three Notes

_____

_____

_____

_____

_____

_____

_____

_____

_____

_____

_____

_____

_____

_____

_____

_____

_____

Accepting Your Greatness

You have been called to greatness. Whether you are rich or poor, whether you have a checkered past or you're living the good life, whether you are burdened by those who oppress you or you are in a position of power, you have been called to greatness.

Do you have your "want to," as we discussed in the last chapter? Do you dream of bringing about positive changes in other people's lives? Do you feel called to fix the things that are broken in our world? Do you want people to say, "There goes a servant of God"?

Perhaps you felt this way when you were younger but circumstances, disappointments, and other people's opinions of you have buried the desire to be great deep within you. No matter how you feel about your qualifications or lack thereof, you're still called to greatness.

But not everyone knows how to be great. The prospect of greatness actually scares many people. The book of Jonah tells the story of how God called Jonah to preach in Nineveh. The thought of preaching to so evil a people frightened him, so he ran. God finally grabbed him with a giant fish and straightened him out in the fish's belly. Then Jonah preached in the city, and they repented. But instead of grasping the greatness God had for him, Jonah went to the edge of town and threw a pity party. Today, experts call it a Jonah complex—a fear of the responsibility that comes with greatness.[9]

Does fear of responsibility, fear of suffering, or fear of hard work keep you from the path of greatness? You're not alone. Let's face it: no one wants to suffer the way Jonah did on his path, or the way David did when he was on the run from King Saul, or the Israelites on their way to the Promised Land (Jonah 1:17; 1 Samuel 23:14; Numbers 32:13). But to achieve the greatness of your God-given purpose, you need to accept what comes with His plan to get you there.

THE CALL

David was just a boy, not a big man like his brothers, when he faced Goliath. He didn't seem like someone destined for greatness, but he did have one trait that set him apart: his willingness to be used by God. He had the "want to."

David would become a king. But before being king, before he was chased by Saul, and before men flocked to him to create an army, he was just a boy. He was a boy about to stand alone before a giant warrior whom the entire army of Israel was afraid to fight. This young shepherd was unflinching in his faith in God and undaunted by those around him:

And David said to Saul, Let no man's heart fail because of him; thy servant will go and fight with this Philistine. And Saul said to David, Thou art not able to go against this Philistine to fight with him: for thou art but a youth, and he a man of war from his youth. And David said unto Saul, Thy servant kept his father's sheep, and there came a lion, and a bear, and took a lamb out of the flock: And I went out after him, and smote him, and delivered it out of his mouth: and when he arose against me, I caught him by his beard, and smote him, and slew him. Thy servant slew both the lion and the bear: and this uncircumcised Philistine shall be as one of them, seeing he hath defied the armies of the living God. David said moreover, The Lord that delivered me out of the paw of the lion, and out of the paw of the bear, he will deliver me out of the hand of this Philistine. And Saul said unto David, Go, and the Lord be with thee.

—1 Samuel 17:32–37

David's desire to stop Goliath came from his firm belief that God would use his meager set of skills to defeat the giant. David could have acted like Jonah and walked away. He could have kept his mouth shut and gone back to tending the sheep. He could have listened to authority and run to safety. Instead, David stood up and was counted as a man of God, willing to put his life on the line for what he knew was right.

God has given you certain talents and gifts, and He has called you to a particular work. He has entrusted you with a job on this planet that only you can do. You're not here by accident. Maybe you will help disadvantaged people or save lives. It may be your calling to improve education or healthcare opportunities. Maybe you will raise a son or daughter who will find a cure for cancer. Whatever God calls you to do, if you have the courage and fortitude to follow this path, you will arrive at a place of greatness.

THE CHOICE

We all may be called to greatness, but only a select few will really accept it. God gives you the choice. You come to a moment when you look at two options: Will you put the effort into developing your talents and investing your gifts for God's glory, or will you let them go to waste? Will you spend time studying God's Word, preparing to live the life He wants you to live? Will you put in the extra work or just flip on the television?

Notice that when you turn on the television, you're watching actors using their talents. You're the bystander, watching others reach for greatness. You have eagle potential, but if you choose to eat chicken feed and live in the coop, you will never be an eagle.

God has given you the choice. He will help you, but He won't force you. You have to accept His call to greatness! David was a shepherd. He didn't look like a warrior. But when God called him to greatness, he showed up, willing to accept it. When you accept your greatness, you won't shrink from hard work, and you won't let difficulties stop you. You will choose to see every obstacle as an opportunity.

Consider, for example, the real-life story of a girl named Tonya. When Tonya was told she couldn't dance with the other girls because she fell over when she tried to twirl, she stumbled home, crying. Her mother noticed she was upset and asked what was wrong. Tonya couldn't hold back her heartache.

"Honey, how badly do you want to dance?" her mother asked.

"I can't imagine not dancing," Tonya replied.

Her mother had a friend whose older daughter danced. With a quick phone call, Tonya's mother arranged to help babysit her friend's kids in exchange for the older daughter giving Tonya a lesson in twirling.

Tonya followed the older girl's instructions and corrected her form. Soon, she could twirl. However, her skills still weren't good enough to dance with the other girls. Determined to continue dancing, Tonya went to the library and looked up tips. She practiced at least two hours a day, sometimes four or more, after school.

Tonya danced in a contest and didn't win, but she received feedback on how to be better. She kept dancing, and opportunities started opening up for her. Today, she has a scholarship at a prestigious dance company to learn ballet. After she graduates from school, she wants to teach dance.

Like David when he heard the taunts of Goliath, if you show up, willing to accept your call to greatness, you will see an opportunity in what others see as an obstacle. You will see the potential for God's work when others see an impossible task.

THE PRICE

Muhammad Ali was the greatest boxer in history. He claimed he was, and his critics and his record agreed. He talked a lot about greatness, and one theme rose to the top: his training. His workout regimen was brutal. And what's worse, he hated training. But he wanted to be the greatest, and he knew what it took to get there. He would need to put in the work. He would have to suffer the pain.[10]

The Apostle Paul suffered for his ministry. He was thrown into prison, beaten, shipwrecked, and chased out of town. Out of that suffering came a mature and successful ministry. What if Paul had wanted to spread the gospel of Jesus Christ among the Gentiles but had not been willing to suffer? It couldn't have been done. If Paul had backed down in the face of adversity and pain, then his ministry would never have happened. Instead, he bore the price of his calling, and the body of Christ was forever changed. Even now, thousands of years later, we are still being instructed by the words the Holy Spirit inspired Paul to write.

It's natural to want the glory of Christ without having to take up your cross, but that's not an option. Jesus said, "If any man will come after me, let him deny himself, and take up his cross daily, and follow me. For whosoever will save his life shall lose it: but whosoever will lose his life for my sake, the same shall save it" (Luke 9:23–24).

The purpose that God has for you doesn't come pain-free. It will involve loss and sacrifice. God will develop your relationship with Him, your character, and your skills through times of hardship. You will learn patience and perseverance. You will learn to trust Him when things aren't easy. Only with toil and suffering will your path to greatness be achieved.

Your comfort isn't the only thing you'll have to sacrifice as you follow God's plan for you. You'll also need to let go of some relationships. Not everyone will support you; some will try to hold you back. When you accept your greatness, other people may resent you. Your commitment may draw attention to their own weaknesses or mistakes. They may want to bring you down to justify their choices.

When David became involved in the battle between the Philistines and Israel, his oldest brother, Eliab, was angry (1 Samuel 17:28). Perhaps he wondered how his little brother, the shepherd, could dare to step on the battlefield and interfere with what was going on when the fighting men of Israel were already present. Perhaps he lashed out at David because he was ashamed of his own lack of courage in failing to meet Goliath's challenge. Whatever the motivation for Eliab's anger, David wasn't deterred (1 Samuel 17:29–30).

Don't allow other people's doubts, prejudices, or envy to keep you from the plans God has for you. Stop inviting those who aren't prepared to go on your journey. Like David, turn away from people who are trying to deter you from your rightful path. Stay on task and keep moving forward.

THE ATTITUDE

There's something else you'll need to sacrifice on the path to greatness: your pride. When you accept your greatness, you need to have the attitude that no job is too low for you. David knew he would be the next king. God had already directed Samuel to anoint him (1 Samuel 16:11–13). David knew that he would become the highest person in the land and be waited on hand and foot, but he didn't go forth to seize the throne right then. He didn't even quit his day job and demand the star treatment in his hometown. He went back to tending sheep. He trusted that God would bring it about in His timing.

When you accept God's greatness, you may not shoot to the highest level right away. Don't lose faith if He directs you to take an entry-level job. Trust God and be patient. Keep praying. Listen to what God tells you to do and accept wherever He sends you. The job you take may not make you a lot of money or be everything you want, but you don't have the full picture of how God is ordering your footsteps.

While David was tending sheep, God was preparing him for future fights. David fought a lion and a bear before he fought a giant (1 Samuel 17:34–37). He fought Goliath before he led other men into battle.

Killing Goliath was only a small part of what God had planned for David. Eventually, He would raise David up to be king. God used David's encounter with Goliath as well as other challenges to sharpen his character, to make him a better man, and to bring him recognition. If others didn't see

David's greatness, they wouldn't support him becoming king.

Remember, where you are is not your final destination. When my friend Maggie was in college, she didn't want anything to do with campus ministry. Originally, she didn't think she had a gift to be a spiritual leader for students. However, when someone called and said that Fisk University students were looking for a minister, she went there to serve. Now she's preaching in prestigious pulpits.

When you're working and struggling in little jobs, having to go back to school, it all has its purpose. God is preparing you for bigger tasks to come.

You may be thinking at this point that greatness doesn't sound so appealing anymore. Is this journey all about pain and hard work and giving things up? Not at all! Although you need to suffer and encounter difficulties or prejudices, God didn't call you just for pain.

Every time you fall, you'll feel the scrapes and bruises, but God will mend the wounds. When your life or your heart breaks into pieces, God will take those pieces and build you into a stronger person. You'll learn that you can rely on Him to pull you through anything, so you can let go of fear. You are a resurrection person! Pain does not destroy you. Sacrifice does not diminish you. You were made to rise up again.

Chapter Four Questions

Question: What is your dream or calling for effecting positive change in the world? What circumstances tend to bury or overshadow that dream? Which of these is the greatest obstacle for you: fear of responsibility, fear of suffering, or fear of hard work?

_____

_____

_____

_____

_____

_____

_____

_____

_____

_____

_____

_____

Question: Compare and contrast Jonah and David. What was God's call for each of these famous biblical figures? How did each man respond?

_____

_____

_____

_____

_____

_____

_____

_____

_____

_____

_____

Question: What is, or could be, the "price" for seeing your dream realized or your calling fulfilled? Why does suffering so often accompany greatness?

_____

_____

_____

_____

_____

_____

_____

_____

_____

_____

Action: Time to work on your attitude! Read and memorize Matthew 20:25–28. In what specific way can you humbly serve this week? Choose a way that you can give up your rights and desires for others (without fanfare or recognition) and follow through on it this week.

Chapter Four Notes

Grasshoppers and Giant-Slayers

Whether you think you can or can't do it, you're right.

—Henry Ford[11]

It was the moment of truth. The Israelites stood on the brink of entering the land of blessing and abundance that God had promised to them. The excitement was building. The wait was almost over.

Moses sent twelve men to get a first look at everything the Israelites' new home had to offer and to see what kinds of people lived there. When they returned, they gave their report:

> *And they told him, and said, We came unto the land whither thou sentest us, and surely it floweth with milk and honey; and this is the fruit of it. Nevertheless the people be strong that dwell in the land, and the cities are walled, and very great: and moreover we saw the children of Anak there. The Amalekites dwell in the land of the south: and the Hittites,*

and the Jebusites, and the Amorites, dwell in the mountains: and the Canaanites dwell by the sea, and by the coast of Jordan. And Caleb stilled the people before Moses, and said, Let us go up at once, and possess it; for we are well able to overcome it. But the men that went up with him said, We be not able to go up against the people; for they are stronger than we. And they brought up an evil report of the land which they had searched unto the children of Israel, saying, The land, through which we have gone to search it, is a land that eateth up the inhabitants thereof; and all the people that we saw in it are men of a great stature. And there we saw the giants, the sons of Anak, which come of the giants: and we were in our own sight as grasshoppers, and so we were in their sight..

—Numbers 13:27–33

THE GRASSHOPPER MENTALITY

The path to greatness is not easy. We already discussed in the last chapter that being great requires suffering and sacrifice. Difficulties are part of the journey. What matters is how you handle them.

The ten spies who gave the bad report of the Promised Land allowed fear of the obstacles ahead of them to call the shots. They saw the enemies they would face and they crumbled. They spoke in fear instead of faith, and their fear spread to the rest of the assembly of the Israelites. They considered themselves grasshoppers, just little insects waiting to be squished by anybody who happened along. They forgot that they were God's people. They forgot how He had protected and provided for them all along. They didn't trust that He could give them this bountiful land as He had promised.

Joshua and Caleb, on the other hand, saw the exact same things as the other spies but gave a different report. They spoke courageously when those around them were trembling in fear. They allowed their faith in God to call the shots. They believed that God was able and willing to deliver on His promise to them. It didn't matter how strong their enemies were; God was stronger.

Inevitably, when God gives you direction and you start toward the goal, people around you will tell you why it can't be done. All those "you can't do this" and "you can't do that" and "look at what is going to go wrong" doubts will try to overwhelm you and push you from God's intended path for your life.

Proverbs 3:5–6 reads, "Trust in the LORD with all thine heart; and lean not unto thine own understanding. In all thy ways acknowledge him, and he shall direct thy paths." The absolute only way to get where God wants you to go and embrace the greatness that He has planned for you is to trust Him. You have to remember that you belong to God. You are one of His children, and He will deliver on His promises to you if you keep the faith.

It's a scary world, and you will see and hear things that intimidate you and make you feel like a little grasshopper. Scripture says that "we walk by faith, not by sight" (2 Corinthians 5:7). No matter what enemies and obstacles you see, you can be sure that God will handle them. You can be confident in moving forward because you know you "can do all things through Christ which strengtheneth [you]" (Philippians 4:13). As Jesus said, "With men this is impossible; but with God all things are possible" (Matthew 19:26).

When you are on God's path, bad reports will come your way, whether it be illness, a financial crisis, or a failing relationship. If you allow these bad reports to control you, then you are already defeated. But if you remember that you serve a God who cannot be defeated, then you will be great.

God has a plan for you, and if He presents you with an opportunity, it's not the time to sit down and figure out if it can be done. Of course it can be done! God wouldn't have brought it to you if it weren't feasible, with Him.

People with a grasshopper mentality focus on the danger present in a situation. They operate from fear and negativity. However, people guided by God can see an opportunity where others see a threat. They see insurmountable obstacles as opportunities for God to do impossible things.

GIANT-SLAYERS AND THE POWER PARADIGM

The grasshopper mentality traps you in the fear of your own limitations, but if you learn instead to put your faith in God's limitless power, then you can become a giant-slayer.

Giant-slayers live by their faith in the power of God. If you are one of Christ's redeemed, then the Holy Spirit of God is in you. "For God hath not given us the spirit of fear; but of power, and of love, and of a sound mind" (2 Timothy 1:7). God's people aren't meant to tremble in the face of difficulty; we're meant to live by our faith in confidence and strength.

In Psalm 121, the psalmist declared, "I will lift up mine eyes unto the hills, from whence cometh my help. My help cometh from the LORD, which made heaven and earth" (Psalm 121:1–2). When we lose faith in God, it's because we forget who He is. God is the Creator of the universe. He made the stars, the moon, the oceans, the dry land, the plants, and all beings. He created life and sustains it. There's nobody and nothing greater than He is. He is above all.

The power of God's Word is unmatched. He said, "Let there be light: and there was light" (Genesis 1:3). All He had to do was say the word "light" and it came into existence. So, when God tells you that He is going to do something, you had better believe it. Like Joshua and Caleb, you need to ignore the naysayers. Why would you believe the doubts of grasshoppers when the Creator of the universe has spoken?

Another key to being a giant-slayer is understanding that God cares about us. He doesn't leave the world He created to fend for itself. He weaves people's lives together to make a story of the world that glorifies Him. He is a loving God who watches out for sparrows and has numbered the very hairs on each of our heads (Matthew 10:29–31). When we pour out our hearts to Him, He listens.

When Hezekiah, a good king of Israel, was about to die, he turned to the wall and wept and prayed to God (Isaiah 38:1–3). God sent the prophet Isaiah back to Hezekiah with the message: "Thus saith the LORD, the God of David thy father, I have heard thy prayer, I have seen thy tears: behold, I will add unto thy days fifteen years" (Isaiah 38:5).

In 2 Kings 4:1–7, we read about how God miraculously provided for a poor widow who was about to lose her sons to slavery because of debt.

Being a giant-slayer doesn't mean that you don't have problems; it means you bring your problems to God. When life seems too much for you to handle on your own, pray to God and have faith that He can and will come through for you according to His will. God never fails, so don't let your troubles defeat you. Face them with confidence, knowing that God has a plan for you and can see you through anything and everything that stands in your way if you choose to walk by faith in Him.

You are a child of God, and He has put you in a position to display His power in your life. When an enemy comes your way, you know that you have the strongest ally there is. As Paul wrote, "If God be for us, who can be against us?" (Romans 8:31). When we're on God's side, "we are more than conquerors through him that loved us" (Romans 8:37).

Shadrach, Meshach, and Abednego refused to worship false gods even though they knew King Nebuchadnezzar would throw them into a fiery furnace if they disobeyed his decree (Daniel 3:8–15). They believed that God would protect them from harm, and He brought them out of the furnace unscathed (Daniel 3:16–29).

God is a deliverer. He is a healer. He is a provider. He blesses us and enriches us in Christ. The Lord said, "My grace is sufficient for thee: for my strength is made perfect in weakness" (2 Corinthians 12:9). Whatever you lack, God can more than make up the difference.

No matter what threatens to hold you back—upbringing, past sins, education, financial difficulties, health problems— God can raise you above your circumstances to a life of greatness. He will open doors for you that you can't even see and enable you to take advantage of the right opportunities. So take all of your cares to Him and remember to give thanks when He steps in and shows you the mighty reach of His arm and the wonderful abundance of His love.

SLAYING EVERYDAY GIANTS

Maybe you're thinking that there's no need for giant-slayers today. There's no territory to rise up and take possession of. After all, you're not going to march over to your neighbor's house and call out, "In the name of the Lord, I take possession of this place!"

We don't live in the same circumstances as the Israelites, but that doesn't mean there aren't giants. We face giants every day, and just because they're commonplace doesn't mean they aren't big.

Let's say God gives you a bit more in a paycheck than you expect. You're able to pay off a bill and give a little more to God than usual. You're encouraged by God's faithfulness. He knew your need, and He provided. In church that night, the preacher asks anyone God has blessed to please stand up and say a word.

You know that God has blessed you, but you're unsure about standing up and sharing the news with everyone. The idea of talking in front of a group intimidates you. What if you say the wrong thing? You've never been good with words. When you tried once before, you had a hard time saying what you meant. You're pretty sure no one understood you, if they could even hear you.

The preacher asks again, "Anyone? Anyone at all? God hasn't blessed a single person?"

A man in the seat behind you, Carl, is on the brink of despair. He's not able to make ends meet, and the school is asking for more money so his son can buy a jersey and play the sport he loves. Carl clutches his head in his hands, not even listening to the preacher. He silently prays, "Lord, my boy is such a blessing. He shares the good news of the gospel with everyone he meets. Lord, I just don't have the funds to make this happen."

He can't pray anymore; he's too choked up. What's the use, anyway? It doesn't seem like God is listening. Maybe there isn't a God at all, and everyone just plays church. Carl knows his faith is shaken and that's probably wrong, but he loves his boy so much and doesn't know what to do.

You don't know that Carl is shaken in his faith over the financial burden he can't overcome. The Holy Spirit is pulling you to speak, but you feel like a grasshopper. You sit in the pew, trying to get the courage to give testimony to the fact that you were given enough money to pay your bills and then some.

"No testimonies?" the preacher asks a final time.

You decide not to think about failing. You're going to walk the path God has given you. You stand.

"Ah, yes, tell us what God has done for you."

You explain the predicament you were in, the overtime you worked, and the small bonus your boss gave you. "Now I can give some of it to the Lord."

You hear a sob behind you, and you see that Carl is crying. In moments, members surround him, and he tells his story. Then he adds, "I'm feeling mighty encouraged to hear God has helped someone else. If I have faith, He will do the same for me."

When the Holy Spirit called you to testify, you overcame your fear of public speaking, and as a result, Carl's faith has been restored. But there is still another giant to slay tonight. You look over at the preacher. He gives a nod, saying with his eyes that putting your money in the offering plate or meeting Carl's needs is up to you and God.

The Holy Spirit gives you clear direction. "Carl," you say in a quiet voice. "That jersey is the amount I have left. Let's get your boy that jersey."

The path of greatness is paved with moments like this, when the Holy Spirit works in your everyday life to help the people around you in the ways He knows they need most. You need to trust that when the Holy Spirit moves you, God is about to do something great. When He is ready to act, let faith carry you and no amount of fear will stand in your way.

Whether you are called to give your testimony, are facing an illness, are trying to provide for your family, or are considering going to another country to serve God, you need to trust Him with your giants. Don't allow your circumstances to intimidate you. Don't let others tell you what you can't do. You may feel like a grasshopper sometimes, but it doesn't matter because the God you serve is great. Nothing is impossible for Him.

Chapter Five Questions

Question: What obstacles make you feel like a "grasshopper"? Are there people in your life who have the "it can't be done" attitude of the ten fearful spies? How do they affect you or others around you?

_____

_____

_____

_____

_____

_____

_____

_____

_____

_____

_____

Question: How can you move from a grasshopper mentality to a giant-slayer mentality? How can you help others who are fearful overcome their hesitations?

_____

_____

_____

_____

_____

_____

_____

_____

_____

_____

Question: When have you seen the Holy Spirit orchestrate circumstances within the body of Christ to meet needs and change lives because of the obedience of a believer in facing their giant?

_____

_____

_____

_____

_____

_____

_____

_____

_____

_____

Action: What you believe about God will make the key difference in how you approach the giants in your life. Looking back through this chapter, you will see several names/attributes of God listed. Write these down, and then add other names/attributes to the list. Put your list in a prominent place where you can read over it often (you may want to use special writing or design something on the computer to make it stand out). Each time you are faced with a giant, remind yourself who God is and why you can trust Him.

Chapter Five Notes

_____

_____

_____

_____

_____

_____

_____

_____

_____

_____

_____

_____

_____

_____

_____

_____

_____

God Works Miracles

Close your eyes and open your Bible to a passage, any passage, and you won't be far from an account of God performing a miracle. God is in the miracle business.

Many people throughout history, and in today's world, offer first-hand accounts of God's intervention. In this age of information and the internet, it takes only a few moments to locate reports of modern-day miraculous healings brought about by prayer and faith.

Have you seen or experienced a miracle? A crash that should have left you crippled, yet you've sustained no injuries? A fire in the kitchen that should have gotten out of control, but the tiny bit of baking soda you had on hand put it out completely?

There are even simpler miracles than those—like falling forward as you start downstairs and feel a hand draw you back, or having time stand still to allow you to make it to a crucial meeting on time when you were running several minutes late.

God doesn't always do miracles. He knows the future, and He knows what is best for us; sometimes that doesn't involve a miracle. But sometimes, His hand is felt in your life, and the experience is unbelievable.

If you don't think you've ever experienced a miracle, have you tried praying for one? Maybe you're not sure if you're doing it right, or maybe you don't have a clue how to begin. Or perhaps it's because you don't *believe* God does miracles.

Regardless, if you're struggling and straining and can't see the way out of your difficult, impossible-seeming situation, be assured there is a miracle already knocking at your door.

A MIRACLE-WORKING GOD

The book of Acts details the spread of Christianity. The message of Christ's resurrection started with the Apostles and became worldwide news in a generation. How?

One reason was that the persecution in Jerusalem expelled the believers out into the world. But the most crucial factor was the Apostles' mission trips. Wherever these followers of Christ went, they preached and performed miracles. The miracles caught people's attention in a big way.

Many believers strong in faith arrived in a city far north of Jerusalem called Antioch, and what started in Jerusalem as a trickle of water became a rushing river in Antioch. The book of Acts, leading up to Paul's imprisonment in chapter 12, describes the river of God's grace growing wider in fulfillment of what He promised. This was the miracle-making God at work.[12]

Later on, Paul and Silas were both locked in prison because they preached a resurrected Christ (Acts 16:19–24). God could have hidden a file in their cell, or a guard who believed could have let them out, but God chose a bigger miracle—an earthquake. Why?

Because He wanted to let everyone know He was still a miracle-working God. He doesn't need your power or resources any more than He needed the help of a guard to let Paul and Silas out. He doesn't need anything from you, except for your willingness to let Him do what He needs to do. If you're living in struggle and strain, in the darkness, God brings the miracle.

GOD'S POWER—MAKING IT HAPPEN

Shortly after Christ died for our sins and rose again—the miracle of all miracles—those who believed were persecuted. Peter, one of the most boisterous and zealous of Christ's disciples, was on King Herod's most-wanted list. He'd already killed James, the brother of John, and as Acts 12 recounts, he captured Peter and put him in prison. The Christian community in the city spread the word about Peter's predicament, and many believers came together to pray for him "without ceasing" (Acts 12:5).

In his cell, Peter awoke to a vision, but it wasn't a dream—it was an angel! The angel told him wake up and get dressed (Acts 12:7–8), and once Peter was ready, he followed the angel out of the cell door (Acts 12:9). They passed the guards, and once they were outside and the iron gates opened, Peter was awake enough to realize he wasn't seeing things (Acts 12:11). He rushed to the house where his fellow Christians were praying and knocked on the door (Acts 12:12–13).

Rhoda, a young believer, answered. It was Peter, the answer to their prayer! (Acts 12:13–14). She ran off to tell the others—leaving Peter waiting on the street, locked out.

The others thought she was crazy. Peter was in prison. They didn't believe the power of their own prayers!

They heard knocking again. They went to check. Yes, indeed, there stood Peter. They opened the door, and he told them all that he had experienced. (Acts 12:16–17)

As you can see clearly in the story of Peter's escape from prison, God has the power to change situations in our lives on earth, and that's ultimately what a miracle is. When it comes to God using His power in miracles, the Bible uses two words to describe His interaction with the human world:

Exousia. God has the authority to change any situation He chooses to.[13]

Dynamis. God has the strength to transform, wreak havoc, and overthrow the schemes of the enemy. This is the root for the English word dynamite.[14]

Given those two definitions, it seems like God would want to use His incredible power to control the galaxies and move nations across the face of the earth. And that He does—but He works in individual lives as well.

In fact, God has miracles for everyone. He is mighty and delivers powerful miracles to touch the lives of people who seem untouchable. God has no shortage of miracles.

FROM DIRE STRAITS TO SPREADING THE GOSPEL

When King Herod killed James and moved to destroy Peter, God delivered His miracle by moving Peter out of Herod's grasp (Acts 12). Even when your enemy seems to have you tied up and thinks you're about to give in, every step he makes to destroy you is just bringing him closer to his own end. As you avoid destruction through God's intervention, it's just another step for God to show how great and full of grace He is.

For every challenge you experience, God has a remedy in place, so don't fret. For every Red Sea, He provides a rod to be stretched out so His people can walk across the dry seabed (Exodus 14:16). For every Pharaoh and his pursuing posse, He supplies a Red Sea to swallow up the enemy (Exodus 16:16–28). For every Jim Crow, God gives us a Rosa Parks, and for every hater, He gives us a Martin Luther King, Jr., with a message of love and freedom.

And when Satan tries to destroy those who bring the gospel, God uses their suffering to spread the message throughout the world, writing it on the hearts of all. When circumstances seem to be at their direst, the miracle is right there, around the corner—or already at the door.

Notice, too, that in Acts 12 God worked more than one miracle: He delivered Peter from prison, but He also disciplined Herod, a king who had perpetrated grievous sins with no apparent remorse. Back in the book of Genesis, Sarah scoffed at the idea of having a child in her old age (Genesis 18:12). Yet, not only did she have a son (Genesis 21:2–3), but from her and Abraham, God also created a people who would eventually show the world His character and their path for salvation. And in their exodus from Egypt, God fed His people with both bread from heaven and quail for meat (Exodus 16). God isn't limited in the number of miracles He can work in one moment!

God's miracle-making knows no bounds because He will do whatever He deems necessary on our behalf. He defends His children, as Saul experienced first-hand when Jesus spoke to him (and left him temporarily blind) on the road to Damascus. There Jesus asked Saul, who had been harassing and hunting His followers, why he was persecuting Him (Acts 9:4–5. As a direct result of this miraculous encounter, Saul turned to Christ and became known as Paul—an Apostle unmatched in his zeal for the gospel, as well as the author of much of the New Testament (Acts 9:20; Acts 13:9).

Miracles are God's way of saying, "Trust Me, I can handle this." Next time you experience pain or struggle, have faith that He'll be right there to lift you up and turn the situation around. Requesting His presence and intervention creates a connection between you and God that allows anything to happen. After all, He is in the miracle business.

ACCEPTING GOD'S MIRACLES

Because God is in the business of miracles, He will show up anytime, anywhere. Remember what happened three days after Jesus died on the cross? Just as everyone believed all hope was gone, God did the impossible: Jesus rose from the dead.

God delivers miracles so you know He can handle your troubles. When things look dark and awful, remember that anything is possible for Him. At the right moment, He will show up and take care of anything that needs fixing. He will transform darkness into a marvelous light (1 Peter 2:9).

Sometimes you won't even recognize a miracle at first. Remember, when Peter was in prison and God came to him, Peter didn't immediately think it was real. He thought he was experiencing an especially realistic dream. In your life, too, God will work some miracles for you that are so awesome, you may not recognize them right away as instances of God acting on your behalf. But afterward, when you look back and reflect, you can see more clearly in hindsight how God carried you through a situation—and then you'll be amazed at His power, goodness, and grace!

But there's a catch: when God works a miracle, you need to respond. When He tells you to get up, get up. When you can't see any way out of a bad situation, instead of having a pity party and feeling sorry for yourself, be on the lookout for God's cue. Peter might not have expected an angel to show up at his prison cell, precisely, but when it happened—and the angel woke him up and told him to get up—he rose to his feet instead of dragging his feet.

And when Peter stood up, the miracle manifested in full. It was after Peter responded to God's presence, in the form of the angel, that his chains fell off (Acts 12:7). Likewise, if you want God to work a miracle in your situation, show Him you are ready to accept His help.

Once you're ready for Him, as Peter was, God will make things happen. He will make doors open for you, just as He did when He led Peter out of the prison. He simply needs you to play your part when the time comes. Then you, too, will experience God's sweet deliverance.

KEEP PRAYING

Your role in God's miracles isn't limited to reaction or response, though. Remember, it's up to you to pray for the miracles *you want to happen*. That last phrase is key, because as strange as it sounds, many people pray for miracles they are *not* looking for—miracles they don't really care about. They'll pray for a million bucks, but there's no real faith or hope behind their words. It's fake.

Don't pray that way! If you pray for people and situations truly close to your heart, sooner or later God will show up and make a miracle happen.

Not far from where I live, some time ago there was a severe drought that lasted for years. Prayers were arranged at the local church, and one of the participants was an old man in a wheelchair with an umbrella.

Other people asked him, "Why did you bring an

umbrella?"

And he replied, "If we are praying for rain, I want to have my umbrella when the rain comes." Not if, but *when*.

When you pray for your miracle, be like the old man with an umbrella: ask for things you truly care about. If a matter is close to your heart, then you'll already be prepared to accept God's miracle in the situation.

Recall that when Peter went to prison, the believers prayed earnestly, without ceasing. They strained beyond the natural and prayed, because although they themselves didn't have the key to let Peter out, they believed that if they directed their request to heaven, God would do what they couldn't do. And God delivered.

So if things get really bad and you can't see any way out of your situation, just keep on praying until God makes His move. Don't give up on your miracle. Remember, Herod the king killed James and imprisoned Peter, and the Jerusalem church was devastated. But they prayed for Peter's release, and as they were praying, Peter stood at their door, knocking. They couldn't believe it was him, at first, but Peter kept knocking until they answered. Then Peter had the opportunity to share his testimony about God's providence and deliverance—as you will, too, regarding the miracles He works in your life.

But miracles start with a prayer and with opening your eyes and ears and see what God is doing for you. Don't forget who you are in the Lord—your authority and your divine connection. When the going gets hard, when you're at the bottom of the darkest pit, get on your knees and pray. If you are a child of God, there is an angel appointed to take care of you: "Are they not all ministering spirits, sent forth to minister for them who shall be heirs of salvation?" (Hebrews 1:14).

Angels and miracles aren't reserved for an Apostle like Paul in the early days of the church. Miracles happen every day—so look for them! Listen for their knock on the door. Pray earnestly, seek God's intervention, and stay true to the path on which He's set you.

God has all power in His hands, and He will transform you. Let Him show you all He has in store for you, even in the midst of your most difficult situations. Ultimately, trust that He will work out all things on your behalf and to His greater glory.

Chapter Six Questions

Question: Have you ever witnessed or experienced a miracle? Describe the situation. How did it build your faith or change your view of God?

_____

_____

_____

_____

_____

_____

_____

_____

_____

_____

_____

Question: Why do you think God allowed the Apostle James to be killed but delivered Peter from prison? What can you learn from their lives?

_____

_____

_____

_____

_____

_____

_____

_____

_____

_____

_____

Question: What is a specific miracle close to your heart that you are praying to see God do? How have you demonstrated your faith that He will act?

_____

_____

_____

_____

_____

_____

_____

_____

_____

_____

Action: Sometimes we fail to recognize the miracles all around us. Each night for one week, write down all the miracles you saw that day. These can be things in your own life or that you observed in others' lives. At the end of the week, review all the many ways in which God was answering prayers and transforming lives.

Chapter Six Notes

_____

_____

_____

_____

_____

_____

_____

_____

_____

_____

_____

_____

_____

_____

_____

_____

Growing in Life's Valleys

Sitting by the bedside of a beloved member of his flock, a preacher listens to her death rattle. She's not awake. Would she even hear him if he reads the passage aloud?

Somewhere else, Daddy picks up the Bible. He, his wife, and their children face bad news. He has cancer, and none of the five children has graduated from high school yet. Prospects don't look good. He fingers the pages and turns to a passage he loves to read. Will he, a grown man scared out of his wits, find comfort?

In a different town, a woman sobs. She lost her job and can't provide for her children. Life has been, in her words, hell on earth since her husband just up and left her and the kids for another woman. She's worked so hard, she can barely stay awake. But now even the work was gone. Her best friend, the one she tells everything to, is the one he ran off with. She opens her Bible, looking for comfort.

One passage of Scripture has been generously used during

times of extreme trials. The passage has been recited by soldiers for millennia as they prepared for battle. Through hardship and loss, amidst destruction and last-ditch efforts for survival, these words have been repeated by believers and unbelievers alike. These few verses are poetry of the highest order—a profound expression of the human capacity for hope and desire for inner peace.

In the King James Version, the psalmist says:

> The LORD is my shepherd; I shall not want. He maketh me to lie down in green pastures: he leadeth me beside the still waters. He restoreth my soul: he leadeth me in the paths of righteousness for his name's sake. Yea, though I walk through the valley of the shadow of death, I will fear no evil: for thou art with me; thy rod and thy staff they comfort me.
>
> **—Psalm 23:1–4**

Have you ever walked through the valley of shadow of death? Do you remember hitting rock bottom? Was there a time when you couldn't take one more problem or one more piece of bad news?

I've been there. You've been there. Everyone has reached a point of crying devastated, grief-stricken tears. Everyone has lain in bed in utter exhaustion. Everyone has suffered complete rejection. Everyone has been bullied, shamed, or terrified at some point. No one is immune to the valleys of life.

But here is what I have learned: the valleys of the shadows of death are in your life because God wants you to absorb important lessons. God wants you to grow.

You know that God has a plan for you. He has carefully constructed the paths of everyone. You may not know why He leads you where He chooses, but there is a purpose in every step. And even when life seems to have taken a turn for the worst—even when you are at the bottom of the darkest pit you can imagine—it's still part of God's plan.

Even so, living in the valley of the shadow of death can seem a nightmare that leaves you feeling as if you'll never wake up. You cannot see the path, the sun is blocked by hills, and feelings of depression and hopelessness roar like wild creatures ready to devour you.

How will you stay on the path during such times?

ALWAYS ON HIS MIND

An ex-convict, Chuck, stumbled along the street. Even though he'd done his time and found forgiveness with Jesus in prison, he didn't know much about God. The ladies at the small church down the road found out he had served jail time and made sure he was shunned. And though he was going straight now, work was hard to find. He had a cheap, noisy apartment. He didn't feel he would ever get his feet under him.

People walked by, so content and so pleased with their lives. They wore warm coats and wouldn't dare put a hat atop such fine haircuts. What were they thinking? Not about him. If they did, it was in disgust.

What if one of these passersby spared a care for him and

actually spent a little time thinking about him? The thought warmed him.

Before Chuck could stop himself, he held a hand out to a well-dressed man. The man's long trench coat reached just above designer shoes.

Chuck walked up to the total stranger and asked the person to think of him for an hour or two. The man reached for his wallet.

"No, no," Chuck said. "I'm serious. I don't want money. I've gotten out of prison and am going straight. I just need someone to think of me for a bit. Believe in me. If I knew there was someone, somewhere thinking of me, I believe I could find myself and turn my life around."

The man put his wallet away. "Sure, kid. I can do that." He started to walk away but then turned back. "Yeah, I'll think of you."

After this, Chuck found the confidence to walk up to a few men unloading trucks and ask for a job. The way he held himself impressed the men, and they hired him.

It's easier to get up, brush the dust off, and go on when someone thinks about and believes in you. But here's the amazing part: someone believes in you twenty-four hours a day, seven days a week, relentlessly: God.

God thinks about you and your path all the time. David knew God thought of him without ceasing, which led him to declare, "Thou preparest a table before me in the presence of mine enemies: thou anointest my head with oil; my cup runneth over" (Psalm 23:5). Simply put, we're God's favorites. The table he lays out is for us, and it's in constant preparation. He fills our cup, and He continues to fill it. God is forever thinking of our welfare.

Even when you're going through a hard time, as David did on many occasions, you always have the Lord as your shepherd. Though your trials feel like they'll last forever, they will one day end, because He is watching out for you.

Does the end to your particular valley end the blessings from the Lord? No! You know you'll continue to graze in green pastures, by still waters, and your soul will be restored.

PAIN WITH A PURPOSE

God gives you valleys for a purpose. You have lessons to learn, and frankly, you're not going to learn them in easygoing times. God puts you in the valley so you can see things you need to work on. There are things in life that you will never learn until you find yourself in a valley.

Teachers know this principle well. Let's face it, schoolwork is a pain more often than not—including for the teachers who have to grade it afterward. So, why do teachers and professors sometimes seem to morph into supervillains, laughing with joy, when they hand out assignments? Apart from the rare instance of sadistic glee, teachers can give their students difficult assignments with a smile on their face because they know that the end result will be positive. If it's a well-considered assignment, by the time the task has been accomplished, the student will be a more knowledgeable and skilled person. Even better, school is a fairly safe environment to learn lessons for life, with teachers imposing carefully designed valleys on students.

Life, however, isn't safe. No one is making sure the events that befall you are rated G by the MPAA. The thrill of new life, the horrors of death, and everything in between are on the schedule for your life—and God is there, every step of the way.

But be warned: God is not the only one in your valley with you, and the experience will show you who your real friends are. In his second letter to Timothy, Paul explained from a prison cell how some of his erstwhile friends had reacted to his difficult circumstances:

> *Do thy diligence to come shortly unto me: For Demas hath forsaken me, having loved this present world, and is departed unto Thessalonica; Crescens to Galatia, Titus unto Dalmatia.*
>
> **—2 Timothy 4:9–10**

If you live long enough, you will know people who smile in your face and stab you in the back. God gives you valleys in part to learn who your true friends and enemies are—and especially, of course, that no one is more dependable than He is in our moments of greatest need.

Your valley can change your whole perspective and make you see things in a different light. God puts valleys in your path to help you learn who you are and know Him more fully. You won't be the same person at the end of the trial you were at the beginning; where you are right now is not where you're going to end up.

LEARNING TO ACCEPT YOUR VALLEYS

God's wisdom awaits you in your valleys, but you must know how to grasp His lessons. You can pretend the lessons aren't there, you can refuse to claim what He's trying to teach you, or you can embrace your valley with the understanding that it's part of God's plan for you. This third option is the way God intends his children to respond. Psalm 23 shows you three ways of responding if you find yourself in a valley:

1. Be wise and blessed to accept the reality of your situation.

2. Be victorious when you announce your response to the valley.

3. Be more than a conqueror when you acknowledge your resources in the context of your valley.

Many people ignore the lessons of their valley because they refuse to acknowledge God's role in them. Alternatively, they may submit to the trials of their valley as a form of punishment because trials are sometimes viewed as consequences for sin. Some people assume a loving God wouldn't help us grow using these methods. Yet if He didn't allow trials in our lives, it would in fact show He didn't love us—that He would be content to let us wallow in our ignorance and inability.

You can take three pots of boiling water, put three different food items in them, and get completely different results. For the 330 million people in America, there are 330 million different responses to valleys. Just as eggs boil hard, some people become hardened and mean. Others, having gone through their valley, will soften and curl up in the corner, like boiled vegetables. But some people are like the boiling water that falls through coffee grounds and transforms into delicious, aromatic, energy-infusing refreshment. People who embrace their valleys of hardship as times of growth in God will come out the other side richer and transformed in a most beautiful way.

Take care not to be an egg or a vegetable. Troubles, trials, and pain can destroy you if you let them. Although you may feel like the situation you're going through is too much for you—too hard, too long—you don't have to crash and burn. A trial that seems too much for you is too much for you, which is God's way of encouraging you to turn to Him (1 Corinthians 10:13).

God has already measured the path for you and knows the trials you will face, and He is aware of your limits. He has given you the opportunity to grow in Him. As Psalm 27:5 says, "For in the time of trouble He shall hide me in His pavilion: in the secret of His tabernacle shall He hide me; he shall set me up upon a rock." There's no need to let the trials destroy you. Psalm 37 likewise assures us, "The steps of a good man are ordered by the Lord: and he delighteth in his way. Though he fall, he shall not be utterly cast down: for the Lord upholdeth him with His hand" (Psalm 37:23–24).

It's best, then, to lean on Him. Instead of merely reciting Psalm 23:4, truly think and reflect on the words, "Yea, though I walk through the valley of the shadow of death, I will fear no evil: for thou art with me; thy rod and thy staff they comfort me."

Through the psalmist's words, God is letting us know, "I have a staff for you to lean on and depend on. The staff is made of perfect divinity—it's Jesus." God gives you all you need to get through the hardest and darkest moments in your life. Call Him; lean on Him. He'll hold you up and bring you through.

Yes, being in the valley is frightening and feels unbearable at times. But God is there with you. He gets under the load that's settled on your shoulders, and He helps you carry it up the hill. God gives you energy and strength for the journey.

He also shifts His position as He walks with you: He leads you on the mountain, He gets behind you when you're growing spiritually, and He is by your side, right with you, when you're going through the worst of the worst—the shadow of death. Trust Him.

COMMUNING WITH GOD IN YOUR VALLEY

God walking by your side though the worst of times means you can talk to Him. Psalm 23 shows us that when things are going well, we tend to talk *about* God, in the third person: "*He* restoreth my soul: *he* leadeth me in the paths of righteousness" (Psalm 23:3, emphasis mine). But when the going gets tough, the narrative shifts to second person because we talk *to* God: "Yea, though I walk through the valley of the shadow of death, I will fear no evil: for *thou* art with me" (Psalm 23:4, emphasis mine).

When your burden gets too heavy, start talking *to* God. He is a Lord you can talk to, for He will hear your faintest cry and answer. One way or another, He will help you in your situation.

Be aware, too, that when you're walking through your valley of shadow, sometimes God sends support through someone else. Don't expect Him to show up in person or send His angel every time. God knows how best to show up in your situation, and He does so at exactly the right time. Sometimes that means a neighbor makes a meal for you while you're sick. Other times, a stranger will know the perfect words to say in an especially difficult moment and you'll feel a calming spirit settle in and around you. At other times, He simply quiets the world and whispers His truths into your heart.

Listen for His gentle voice and look for His ministering angels. But also appreciate those in the church who show God's love to you in your valleys. They're just as important, if not more so, than the angels. A brother or sister in Christ is a powerful help in times of trouble (Psalm 46:1). As Jesus said, "For where two or three are gathered together in my name, there am I in the midst of them" (Matthew 18:20).

Never forget that God has given you your valley to help you see things you need to work on. He wants you to grow and flourish. He wants you to move forward and learn how to bloom wherever you planted. This is why James wrote,

"My brethren, count it all joy when you fall into various trials, knowing that the testing of your faith produces patience" (James 1:2–3 NKJV). A valley is not the occasion for a pity party, but a time to learn from your trials.

Valleys will have you going to church when you said you wouldn't go anymore. Valleys will have you on your knees praying when you promised not to say another word to God. Valleys will have you up all night searching the Scriptures when you've not picked up your Bible in years.

Valleys will show you the power of God.

Thank Him no matter what happens in your life. God's plan for you is forward progress, not a stagnant life. Choose wisely how you respond to those valleys He has prepared for you. Trust Him and lean on Him. He is an awesome God who keeps you, provides for you, leads you, and guides you. You will come out at the other end spiritually stronger, more mature, and closer than ever to your Lord.

Chapter Seven Questions

Question: Describe a time when you walked through a dark and difficult "valley." (Perhaps you are there now.) How does it change your perspective to know that the Lord is always thinking of you and shepherding you through the valley?

_____

_____

_____

_____

_____

_____

_____

_____

_____

_____

_____

Question: What are some ways that people respond to valleys? What should a believer's response be?

_____

_____

_____

_____

_____

_____

_____

_____

_____

_____

Question: Do you do more talking *about* God or *to* God? What is the significance of this shift in Psalm 23? What are some of the ways suffering has changed you and your perspective?

_____

_____

_____

_____

_____

_____

_____

_____

_____

_____

_____

Action: Is there someone in your church or community who is going through a "valley"? Plan and prepare a practical and intentional way you can encourage them this week.

Chapter Seven Notes

God Deserves Your Thanks

God redeemed you from eternal punishment with His sacrifice on the cross. He set right the wrongs in your life. He walks by your side in valleys and on mountaintops. You know you've done nothing to deserve such a faithful guide, a gentle friend, someone who loves you enough to chastise you and shows you how to grow.

So, what happens now?

The psalmist explains that God "is good: for His mercy endureth forever" (Psalm 107:1). This is the pattern for the rest of your life: God continues to be there, every step of the way!

He wants you to grow and to flourish. That's why He gives you valleys—so you can learn and progress. Moreover, when you're going through the valley of the shadow of death, God walks by your side. And if you're wandering lost in the wilderness, hungry and thirsty, with your soul faltering, He comes to your rescue. He lifts you out of any and every bad situation because He is good and merciful without fail.

The question then becomes: how do you respond to the gift of such a God as your Father, Lord, and Savior?

The answer: with eternal thanksgiving—praising Him with every fiber of your being and your life.

KNOWING THE LORD

Psalm 107 is a call to praise God. But how can you praise someone if you don't know who He is or what He has done?

Imagine getting a package on your front step that's a bit strange, and you're grateful, but you don't know whom to thank. It's a rolling pin. Interesting.

Later in the day, the kids are starved for biscuits and you want to make them from scratch like your mom used to make, but you don't have a rolling pin.

Wait a moment! Someone had set a rolling pin by your front door. You can make biscuits from scratch after all!

Whether you realized it or not at the time, you've no doubt experienced moments when you, or someone close to you, was freed from a trap or healed from the sickbed by God. Without God, you or the other person would be dead or destroyed, whether physically or emotionally, but because He came to the rescue, now you can appreciate more precious moments together with your loved ones.

Sometimes, full appreciation of a gift from God can't always be realized in the moment, and if you don't know God, you'll forever wonder who gave it to you. For example, maybe you used to have a temper, but through some valleys and hard times, you can now control your emotional responses. You know this transformation wasn't a simple choice or flip of a switch on your part, because your temper had been out of control before. It was a gift—and you must recognize *who* gave it to you and *why*.

You must know God to have a relationship with Him, to be delivered by Him, and to praise Him. The psalmist said:

> *Then they cried unto the Lord in their trouble, and he delivered them out of their distresses. And he led them forth by the right way, that they might go to a city of habitation. Oh that men would praise the Lord for his goodness, and for his wonderful works to the children of men!*
>
> *—Psalm 107:6–8*

God steers you the right way every time if you get to know Him, learn to listen to Him, and change your ways to follow His leading. Knowing who He is and what He's doing will bring a cry of praise to your lips. Time and again, despite the missteps and misbehavior of the people of Israel and Judah, they would call on the Lord in times of need and recommit themselves to their relationship with Him—and He would deliver them. So it is with you! That's worth a hearty "amen," don't you think?

ON THE RIGHT PATH

Let's face it—everyone gets into situations from which only God offers the only hope of rescue. Only the hand of God can fix some problems. Sometimes we sin and have no recourse but to fall to our knees, knowing full well what we did wrong and praying our life won't be destroyed.

I've been there, too. When I was living in Detroit, I was on a path leading to destruction and death. I thought I was going to die young, but my mother back home was praying for me. And God redeemed me.

Praise God, through God's grace and the prayer of others, I was saved from the path of destruction. God directed my path to Him. As the proverb says, "He shall direct thy paths" (Proverbs 3:6). I'm a living example of this promise, and God will rescue you like He has rescued me. He will put you in a place where you can't lose your way.

I know the one who rescued me, the giver of my most precious gifts, and I pray you do as well. When He frees you, heals you, restores you, and sets you on the right path, remember the deep, overwhelming gratitude that the psalmist expressed when he called for the children of God to thank Him:

> Then they cried out to the Lord in their trouble, and He saved them out of their distresses. He brought them out of darkness and the shadow of death, and broke their chains in pieces. Oh, that men would give thanks to the Lord for His goodness, and for His wonderful works to the children of

men! For He has broken the gates of bronze, and cut the bars of iron in two.

—Psalm 107:13–16 (NKJV)

It's also important to thank God for the predicaments from which He rescues you. Because of my trials and His intervention, I'm better able to tell you that He is faithful, and these words of praise come from my heart into the world: *Thank You and praise You, Jesus!* I cannot help it, because I know where I was headed before He saved me from myself— and how far it would have been from the new path of purpose He has set me on.

Life is a journey, and trials will inevitably happen. It's good to know that you have Jesus, who returns you back to safety, freedom, health, and the blessing of a relationship with your Lord. God is abundantly worthy of our praise, and you can join me in praising Him joyfully!

THANK GOD FROM A TO Z!

I'll repeat it again: you have plenty in your past, present, and future for which to be grateful to God. But in case you fall short of ideas, here is a list from A to Z that covers many of the basics: Thank God...

A – for the Acceptance with which He receives you

B – for His Bounty

111

C – for the Calmness He brings

D – for Deliverance from evil

E – for His Election of the believer to eternal life

F – for the Fullness of Christ

G – for His Grace

H – for the Hope that Christ brings

I – for your eternal Inheritance

J – for the unquenchable Joy of knowing of Jesus

K – for His Kingdom that can't be overturned

L – for His Love that can never be darkened

M – for His Mercy that endures forever

N – for His persistent Nearness

O – for His Omnipresence

P – for His undefiled Purity

Q – for His impenetrable Quietness

R – for His untarnished Righteousness

S – for Salvation that can never be cancelled

T – for Christ's unclouded Triumph

U – for our inseparable Union with Him

V – for the eternal Victory He offers

X – for the eXcellence we can achieve in Him

Y – for our inexhaustible Yearning for God

Z – and for the Zeal for Him with which He fills our hearts.

Followers of Christ have a mantra: "God is good all the time, and all the time, God is good." It's easy to praise the Lord when things are going well. But even when you're down in the dumps, when you're going through your valley of the shadow of death, *God is still good*. Remember, He will allow you to encounter some hardship to help you learn important lessons—and ultimately, to show you just how good He is. Yet God also carries you through valley situations.

When things are going well, don't forget *why* they're going well. God was the one who rescued you and made a difference in your life.

GOD IS THE SOURCE OF BLESSINGS

It's crucial never to forget where the goodness in your life comes from.

Sometimes it's easy to imagine you've woven through your struggles using your own wits and skills. Did you catch the pop fly to make the final out so your team could win the baseball game? You probably feel like a hero in that moment—and maybe you've already forgotten that just before the bat connected with the ball, you were praying to God that He would help you and guide your actions.

Have you ever been unsure how to encourage a friend or family member, but as you struggle for words, you manage to stumble across the exact thoughts they need to hear? You can either thank God for the words He gave you or pretend you're amazing and think far better of yourself than you ought.

113

You may not even realize how much you owe God. "His mercy endureth forever," the psalmist declared (Psalm 136:1). And likewise, 1 Chronicles 16:34 exhorts us, "O give thanks unto the LORD; for he is good; for his mercy endureth for ever." Mercy is what you need more than anything else. For all your failings and mess-ups, you need God's mercy to rescue you *and* transform you. Once you recognize how much you need to lean on His mercy, it's easy to be grateful to God for all He has done for you.

So praise the Lord for what you've received from Him. The Lord has raised you, blessed you, and made a way for you. Maybe He's found a job for you, brought your child back home, or kept food on your table.

If this is the case, the Bible says you should talk about it! You should praise God for what He has done for you. Let others know that God has been good to you. Give Him praise. Even if nobody else is willing to step forward, be strong and offer your testimony—say, "Thank You, Lord!"

God shows up and helps you even when you don't deserve it, when you haven't earned it, when you're unappreciative, and when you've breached your end of the contract. His mercy works on your behalf because this is God's character. God loves you and extends His goodness and His compassion to you. Your Lord gives you another chance. He protects you. He wakes you up every morning, prepares the way for you, and fights your battles for you.

And of course, God specializes in rescues that seem impossible. He performs miracles. He has brought you out of your worst mess-ups and tightest spots like nobody else could.

I have many "nobody but God" moments in my life. Nobody but God could have fixed my finances. Nobody but God could have put me on my feet. Nobody but God could have healed my sick body or wiped tears from my eyes. I'm here to tell you: God has come to my rescue, and He comes to your rescue.

For that, I'm giving Him an offering of thanksgiving. Be sure you're thanking Him for your "nobody but God" moments, too.

Chapter Eight Questions

Question: Along with your eternal salvation, what are some specific ways God has rescued you? Redeemed you? Restored you? Freed you? Healed you? Guided you?

_____

_____

_____

_____

_____

_____

_____

_____

_____

_____

_____

Question: When have you been tempted to take the credit for something that God did in and through you? How can you give Him the glory for your success?

_____

_____

_____

_____

_____

_____

_____

_____

_____

_____

Question: What are some of the "nobody but God" moments in your life? How have you thanked God for these? How have you given public testimony to His goodness to you in these areas—or how might you do so now?

_____

_____

_____

_____

_____

_____

_____

_____

_____

_____

_____

Action: Take time to do as the old song says and "count your blessings." Then publicly share what you are thankful for with your family and/or church family. As you set this tone of gratitude to God, it will encourage others to do the same!

Chapter Eight Notes

The Path of Faith

Every believer in God has been given a path to greatness. You're a giant-slayer, not a grasshopper. You will be bold in your decisions to do right. You will step out on faith when the Lord leads. You now know that by trusting in Him, you can slay any Goliath that steps in your way (1 Samuel 17).

God-given, God-driven love propels you on this path. If you're still uncertain whether your faith is worth your time, commitment, and sacrifice, consider that your faith in God goes hand in hand with your love for God—and keeps you moving in the direction He intends for you.

And the Lord also guides and provides for you as you keep moving forward. He delivers on every promise, and as you walk, you'll encounter opportunities and miracles of His making.

Experiencing these blessings, though, takes thoughtful interaction with God. Pray to Him and talk with Him. Ask for His wisdom and intervention. Don't be afraid of making requests, large and small.

Don't be discouraged, either, by the fact that others will try to slow you down on your path to greatness in God. Letting their jealousy bump you from the path is easy to do if you take your eyes off the Lord.

Likewise, maintain your focus and your faith when you encounter seasons of trial. God allows such valleys to encourage growth. These difficult times are essential in sculpting who you are in Christ—in preparation for greater things ahead.

Thankfully, anywhere along your path, you can call on Him for support. Whenever you call on Him in good faith, you can depend on Him to help and guide you. He is always looking out for you and will come to your rescue, without fail, when you need Him and open yourself up to His aid.

So, what's the verdict? Is your faith worth it? Will you trust and lean on God to lead you down your path to greatness in Him—the path of faith? Or will you settle for second best?

ON GOD'S SIDE

In times of difficulty and uncertainty, God "is good, a stronghold in the day of trouble; and He knoweth them that trust in Him" (Nahum 1:7). In a world where nothing is guaranteed—where destitution or death can come suddenly and unexpectedly, and where violence and wickedness of all kinds runs amok in our streets, in our news reports, in our web browsers, and in our entertainment—"the name of the

LORD is a strong tower: the righteous runneth into it, and is safe" (Proverbs 18:10).

When you struggle to trust, when you feel like you're all alone and left to your own devices, take time to read and reflect on these promises from God:

- He exercises His power through you. (Luke 24:49)

- He offers you communion and companionship. (John 14:21, 23)

- He answers your prayers. (John 15:7)

With God by your side, you may be "troubled on every side, yet not distressed ... perplexed, but not in despair; persecuted, but not forsaken; cast down, but not destroyed." (2 Corinthians 4:8–9).

Christian life is far from easy by modern standards. Living by God's principles requires courage and strength, but God never leaves you to fend for yourself.

He takes care of you while you're toiling. When you're tired and feel like you can't take it anymore, you can lean on the arms of your powerful Savior, who holds all power in heaven and earth.

But those who wait on the LORD shall renew their strength; they shall mount up with wings like eagles, they shall run and not be weary, they shall walk and not faint.

—Isaiah 40:31 (NKJV)

When you're lost, He gives you His guidance and leads you. He walks with you and carries you when the going is toughest. If you're surrounded by enemies, He will revive you, stretching forth His hand against your enemies and saving you (Psalm 138:7).

For those who follow Him, God offers eternal rewards. Joining Him on the path of faith and greatness means you will belong to "a chosen generation, a royal priesthood, an holy nation, a peculiar people; that ye should shew forth the praises of him who hath called you out of darkness into his marvelous light" (1 Peter 2:9). You will receive the ultimate reward of rejoicing in his house forever, "for ye shall be a delightsome land" (Malachi 3:12).

He redeems your past, gives your present life meaning, and secures your future forever. And while you walk on His path, you will be lifted and transformed.

ACCEPT GOD'S BLESSING

Knowing all of this, choose God's side today if you haven't already. Truly choose Him to be the center of your path and accept His blessing. Live His Word every day and night, every second of your life. Live His love. Be blessed by His grace and His mercy. God is offering you another chance at a life lived well, in faith and in everlasting, forgiving, all-encompassing love for eternity.

Don't wait any longer. Use the advice I've shared with you here to claim your Christian self. There will never be a better moment. Take this opportunity to receive God and His blessing, leaning on Him in all you are and in all you do—so that in Him you will not perish but will have everlasting life. Amen!

About the Author

In December 1949, Marvin Alphonza Jennings became the second child born to Pastor James and Mrs. Bertha Jennings, and he was their only living child at the time. Marvin graced their home with life and love. Eight siblings followed his birth, seven of whom are now living.

Marvin's parents made sure they provided a Christ-centered home, which fostered strong faith principles in each child. Because of these strong principles, Marvin showed increasing interest in Bible reading and Scripture memorization. At age seven, he invited Christ into his life, and by age sixteen, he was being asked to speak at youth banquets and services. Marvin's love for the Lord and God's Word grew. He knew there was a calling on his life but refused to acknowledge it until after high school graduation. In 1968, Marvin acknowledged and accepted his call to the ministry under his father's pastorate at New True Vine Baptist Church in Detroit, Michigan; two years later, on October 18, 1970, he was ordained.

Marvin met his wife, Janis, at a Youth Day banquet in 1968, where he was the speaker. On July 24, 1971, they were married, and a month later, he was called to pastor a small storefront church, New Birth Missionary Baptist, in Detroit, Michigan. Over time, the Lord added a quiver-full to Marvin and Janis's family: Marvin Jr., Micah, Celestine, Michella, and Calista. Later in their lives, they added two sons-in-law, two daughters-in-law, and fifteen grandchildren. Pastor Jennings is renowned for his love of God, his family, and God's people.

On November 6, 1977, Marvin was called to pastor Second Baptist Church in Bay City, Michigan, the county's oldest black church. In 1978, the church paid off an $11,000 balance on 16.9 acres of land in Essexville, Michigan. In December 1978, Second Baptist broke ground to build a new church on a portion of the land to accommodate their growth, and the structure was completed in September 1979.

After serving eight years at Second Baptist, with much prayer,

Pastor Jennings, Janis, and their children moved to Flint, Michigan. Adhering to God's lead and His plan, in December 1985, Pastor Jennings began pastoring Grace Emmanuel Baptist Church, in Flint, Michigan, where the organizing pastor, Lindell L. Brady, was retiring. After coming to Grace Emmanuel, Pastor Jennings developed and held its first Strategic Planning workshop in 1990, with a group of leaders, ministers, and laypersons. A mission statement, goals, and ministries were developed to meet the needs of the congregants and the community more effectively. From 1995 to 1996, Pastor Jennings began and completed a three-phase building project to accommodate ministry needs and growth. Pastor Jennings pastored Grace Emmanuel Baptist Church for over thirty-four years.

Pastor Jennings has kept these fundamental principles before his church family: to exalt the Savior, evangelize the lost, educate and equip the saints, embrace godly living, and elevate society. He is a man who loves God and God's people and is committed to preaching the gospel of Jesus Christ.

Pastor Jennings's high school years were spent at Phillip Murray/Wilbur Wright Co-operative School in Detroit, Michigan, from which he graduated in June 1968. For three years, he attended the University of Detroit in the Project 100 program. Several years later, Pastor Jennings enrolled at Grand Rapids Baptist College and Seminary, where he earned his Bachelor of Arts degree in May 1985. By January 1988, Pastor Jennings had his Master of Business Administration in Church Management from the Graduate Theological

Foundation. In 2016, he received an Honorary Doctor of Divinity degree from Saint Thomas Christian University, Jacksonville, Florida. From April 17 to 29, 2003, Pastor Jennings attended the Governance Institute (leadership conference for trustees, physicians, and executives) in Chicago, Illinois. In September 2009, he completed Dave Ramsey's Financial Peace University Workshop.

Pastor Jennings has served on several committees and boards and has supported many community groups, including: Hurley Medical Center Board, Flint, Michigan, 2002–2005; Concerned Pastors for Social Action 2004 (president); Great Lakes Baptist District Association, Flint, Michigan (first vice-moderator at large); Mr. Rogers Board (boys' program); One Church One School Program; first Grand Blanc High School Strategic Planning Committee, Grand Blanc, Michigan; Governor Jennifer Granholm's Insurance Project (to provide insurance for urban areas) and her Faith-Based Advisory Council of Flint, Michigan; Amachi Big Brothers/Big Sisters, Flint, Michigan (board member); Grace Emmanuel Economic Community Outreach CDC (president); and the Michigan State Police Caution program. Pastor Jennings was also appointed a chaplain for the Genesee County Sheriff's Office and, in March 2015, was certified as a chaplain for the Flint Police Department.

Over the years, Pastor Jennings has had many honors bestowed on him, including: Grateful Gavel Award, 1995; Urban League Youth Development Award, 1995; Mr. Rogers Just Say No Program, 1996; Martin Luther King Drum

Major Award, 2000–2001; Pastor of the Year Award from the Wolverine State Congress, 2002; Career Alliance Inc. Workforce Development Board of Directors honorary certificate, 2005; AC Lee Faith Community Business and Education Leadership Awards; McLaren Health Care Renowned Community Activist Award, 2014; and Alpha Kappa Alpha Sorority (Zeta Beta Omega Chapter) honors for "Men Making a Difference." The Genesee District Library also honored Pastor Jennings during their annual Black History recognition for making a difference in the Flint Community. In October 2003, the Flint PanHellenic Council saluted Pastor Jennings for outstanding commitment to the city in the area of religion.

Pastor Jennings is known and recognized as a spiritual motivator and educator. He has been the keynote speaker at the 2005 first annual Healthcare Scholarship Ball and at many other businesses, organizations, schools, and churches. He has served as a church growth consultant.

About Renown Publishing

Renown Publishing was founded with one mission in mind: to make your great idea famous.

At Renown Publishing, we don't just publish. We work hard to pair strategy with innovative marketing techniques so that your book launch is the start of something bigger.

Learn more at RenownPublishing.com.

Notes

[1] McAlvany, Donald. "Fellowship of the Unashamed." McAlvany Intelligence Advisor. https://mcalvanyintelligenceadvisor.com/fellowship-unashamed.

[2] McAlvany, "Fellowship of the Unashamed."

[3] Turner, Tina. "What's Love Got to Do with It." Track 2, *Private Dancer*. Capitol, 1984.

[4] Guzik, David. "1 Corinthians 13 – Agape Love." Enduring Word Bible Commentary. Enduring Word, 2013. https://enduringword.com/bible-commentary/1-corinthians-13.

[5] Ingersoll, Karl. "The Breakdown." Faithlife Sermons. https://sermons.faithlife.com/sermons/6015-the-breakdown.

[6] *Encyclopaedia Britannica,* "Abraham Lincoln." By Richard N. Current. April 8, 2018. https://www.britannica.com/biography/Abraham-Lincoln.

[7] Jay, Meg. "The Secrets of Resilience." Wall Street Journal. November 19, 2017. https://www.wsj.com/articles/the-secrets-of-resilience-1510329202.

[8] Oggs, Allan C. *You Gotta Have the Want-To.* Word Books, 1987.

[9] Maslow, A. H. *The Farther Reaches of Human Nature.* Penguin, 1993.

[10] "Muhammad Ali: 'The Greatest' Quotes." Biography. May 31, 2017. https://www.biography.com/news/muhammad-ali-quotes.

[11] Andersen, Erika. "21 Quotes from Henry Ford on Business, Leadership and Life." Forbes. May 31, 2013. https://www.forbes.com/sites/erikaandersen/2013/05/31/21-quotes-from-henry-ford-on-business-leadership-and-life.

[12] Hughes, R. Kent. *Acts (ESV Edition): The Church Afire.* Crossway, 2014.

[13] *Strong's Exhaustive Concordance of the Bible,* "G1849 – exousia." By James Strong. In Blue Letter Bible. https://www.blueletterbible.org/lang/lexicon/lexicon.cfm?t=kjv&strongs=g1849.

[14] *Strong's Exhaustive Concordance of the Bible,* "G1411 – dynamis." By James Strong. In Blue Letter Bible. https://www.blueletterbible.org/lang/lexicon/lexicon.cfm?t=kjv&strongs=g1411.